Western Iowa
Prehistory

Duane Anderson

Illustrated by Lennis Moore

Iowa State University Press, Ames, Iowa

DUANE ANDERSON is director of the Sanford Museum and Planetarium, Cherokee, Iowa. He received his B.A., M.A., and Ph.D. degrees from the University of Colorado — Boulder, specializing in archeology and museum studies. His main interests include research on the culture history of the plains border, museum education and public archeology.

LENNIS MOORE holds a B.A. degree in art education from Luther College, Decorah, Iowa. He is presently serving as an artist and teacher with a Title III E.S.E.A. project entitled "Exploring the Tangible World" being conducted by the Sanford Museum in cooperation with the Cherokee Community School District.

Cover design: front, side and back views of a catlinite amulet described in Chapter 3.

Type composition by the Times Publishing Company, Cherokee, Iowa.

© 1975 The Iowa State University Press
Ames, Iowa 50010. All rights reserved

Printed by
The Iowa State University Press

First edition, 1975
Second printing, 1978

Library of Congress Cataloging in Publication Data

Anderson, Duane, 1943-
    Western Iowa prehistory.

    1. Indians of North America—Iowa—Antiquities. 2. Iowa—Antiquities. I. Title.
E78.I6A52   970.4'77   74-22166
ISBN 0-8138-1765-X

Facsimile Edition International Standard Book Number: 0-8138-2223-8

Contents

Preface

This book was written for the people of western Iowa—laymen, history buffs, teachers and students. It is intended as a general reference and source book. It carries also an urgent plea for the preservation of artifacts and sites for we know very little about the people who came before us. What we do know is based on our knowledge of the objects made and left behind by groups of hunters and farmers who occupied the prairies from the close of the last Ice Age to the Protohistoric Period. For a variety of reasons, these remains are rapidly disappearing.

Further, the little we do know is not widely disseminated. Most people are only vaguely aware of the rich and interesting background of western Iowa. Even Iowa school children are more likely to grow up learning more about Pueblo Indians or Eskimo than people native to their own region. Some information is available at present, but it is mostly inaccessible, locked up in scientific reports, often rather technical, or appearing in other somewhat obscure places.

In reconstructing the story of the past archeologists are seriously handicapped by the nature of the available data. Certainly there are more to cultures than bones and rocks, but often these are about all archeologists have to work with. They have no way of knowing what language a given prehistoric group spoke or to which "tribe" they belonged. Customs and the social order can be reconstructed in only the most general terms. Nevertheless, cultures are patterned. The concepts held in common by a group are reflected to a degree in the things they made. People had to deal with their environment, one another, and with the world of spirits. Different sorts of artifacts resulted from their need to cope with all these areas. With this in mind, it is the job of archeologists to see what they can learn about the extinct social systems of these peoples. As one can see, there is more to archeology than collecting "relics."

Most of the material in this book is drawn from work that has been done over the past twenty to thirty years. The reader should be aware that prehistoric studies were initiated by pioneer archeologists in western Iowa more than a century ago. As elsewhere, archeology in Iowa had its roots in the antiquarian studies of the latter part of the 19th Century. J.B. Cutts reported on ancient relics in northwestern Iowa as early as 1873. Work began along the Des Moines River in the 1880's and 90's when Charles Aldrich and William Williams began reporting on the artifacts and mounds in Webster County. In southwestern Iowa Seth Dean and S.V. Proudfit investigated remains now associated with the Glenwood culture. Soon after, Theodore Lewis reported on stone monuments in north-west Iowa and adjacent Minnesota and Frederick Starr dug into an extensive Oneota site in Lyon County. Starr emerged as one of the most important researchers in the early period. Before the turn of the century he published a bibliography of work done in the state as well as a county-by-county summary of what was known. In 1904 Duren Ward investigated a mound in Dickinson County on which he and two of his associates later reported. The Sioux City Academy of Science and Letters became active in the early 1900's when H.C. Powers and W.T. Stafford excavated a Mill Creek site in Plymouth County. At this time activity in central Iowa included T. Van Hyning's excavations at a spectacular Woodland mound located near Boone.

Charles R. Keyes and his assistant, Ellison Orr, dominated the archeological scene from 1921-1951. The State Historical Society placed Keyes in charge of the Iowa Archeological Survey in 1921 and he began bringing together all existing information. Much of his early work involved searching and compiling but very little digging. Keyes was a remarkably good man for the job. During his thirty years with the survey, he laid the groundwork for contemporary research.

In 1938 Mildred Mott and MacKinlay Kantor, working under Keyes, excavated two Woodland mounds near Webster City. At the same time, Ellison Orr began digging ten Woodland mounds and twelve earthlodges with a federal Work Projects Administration (WPA) crew in Mills County. Orr also surveyed the Glenwood area and recorded many new sites. During the late 1920's and early 1930's, Nestor Stiles, Cherokee, and F.L. Van Voorhis, Alta, were actively recording sites and assembling collections of artifacts. By 1939 Van Voorhis retired and began excavating two Mill Creek earthlodges in Buena Vista County. His work continued until 1942. Ellison Orr conducted more extensive excavations at a Mill Creek site in Plymouth County in 1939, again with a WPA crew. Although some work was accomplished in surrounding areas into the 1940's, very little took place in western Iowa until after 1950. Some references to these pioneer efforts are listed at the end of the Preface. Others appear at the end of appropriate chapters under "Sources and Suggested Readings."

The present era of investigation began in the early 1950's with the establishment of research programs at the University of Iowa, Iowa City, and the Sanford Museum. Along with these developments came the founding of the Iowa Archeological Society and the first of its affiliated chapters. Later the University of Wisconsin began working in northwestern Iowa conducting studies of climatic change, and Iowa State University, Ames, began extensive survey and salvage in the central part of the state. Additional work has been done by the University of Nebraska and the Smithsonian Institution. The principal investigators and the work they accomplished are identified at the end of each of the subsequent chapters.

Throughout the history of western Iowa archeology one of the most neglected areas of inquiry has been the physical remains of the people themselves. To demonstrate the potential of these studies, man's biology is considered in the first chapter. The story of western

Iowa's extinct cultures begins in Chapter 2. The earliest hunters were nomadic peoples who were living in this area thousands of years before the construction of the first pyramids of Egypt. The following chapter on the first pottery makers opens with the introduction of new religious concepts and new economic systems. These Woodland peoples, often called "mound builders," paved the way for settled life in Iowa.

Chapters 4 through 7 tell the story of the cultures of the Late Prehistoric Period when people became village farmers. They were the Great Oasis, Glenwood, Mill Creek and Oneota. From culture to culture there are many similarities in the tools they used, animals they hunted and plants they raised. But on close examination we find that they were distinctly different. Some apparently coexisted peacefully; others were at least occasionally at war. Most disappeared from the record before the dawn of history, but the Oneota survived to meet the European intruders. Thus, they ended 700 successful years of prehistory and began 300 years of hard times under government rule. In Chapter 8 a few words are said about cultures in regions adjacent to western Iowa. Here, particular emphasis is placed on the Late Prehistoric Period when differences are most obvious. If the reader finds this story of the past interesting, it is hoped that he or she will assist archeologists in doing what must be done to insure that our understanding of prehistory is fully developed. Some of the ways the public can help are outlined in the final chapter.

I am grateful to Lennis Moore for his efforts in preparing the illustrations for this book. All items that appear herein are drawn from documented specimens—most of which are in the collections at the Sanford Museum in Cherokee. All illustrations, except for some human bones in Chapter 1, are drawn actual size unless otherwise indicated.

I thank Patricia Williams for reading and typing two drafts of the manuscript. She also researched site locations for the generalized site distribution maps that accompany the text. Others who helped in various ways include Carol Anderson and Sandra Moore.

Although several archeologists have contributed to my thinking, I would like to mention particularly David M. Gradwohl, David A. Baerreis, Dale R. Henning, Adrian D. Anderson, John S. Sigstad, Richard Shutler, Jr. and Marshall B. McKusick. Special thanks must go to Dr. Gradwohl for his efforts in reviewing the manuscript prior to publication. Other subject matter specialists who have shaped my opinions include Mildred Mott Wedel, W.D. Frankforter and Holmes A. Semken. Editorial assistance and a good deal of understanding was extended by Iowa State University Press. It is my hope that my colleagues will find my rather speculative treatment of western Iowa prehistory at least "tolerable," and that the general public will find the subject totally irresistible. The success of archeology in the future will depend in large measure on the interest, support and cooperation of everyone!

Duane Anderson

Sources and Suggested Readings

CUTTS, J.B. (1873), Ancient Relics in Northwestern Iowa. Annual Report of the Smithsonian Institution, 1872, p. 417.

KEYES, CHARLES R. (1920), Some Materials for the Study of Iowa Archeology. Iowa Journal of History and Politics, Vol. 18, pp. 357-370.

KEYES, CHARLES R. (1925), Progress of the Archeological Survey in Iowa. Iowa Journal of History and Politics, Vol. 23, pp. 339-352.

KEYES, CHARLES R. (1927), Prehistoric Man in Iowa. Palimpsest, Vol. 8, No. 6, pp. 185-229.

LEWIS, THEODORE H. (1890), Some Stone Monuments in Northwestern Iowa and Southwestern Minnesota. American Anthropologist, Vol. 3, pp. 269-274.

POWERS, H.C. (1910), Opening of an Indian Mound near Sioux City, Iowa. Records of the Past, Vol. 9, pp. 309-311.

STAFFORD, W.T. (1906), Results of the Investigation of the Indian mound at Broken Kettle Creek. Proceedings of the Academy of Science and Letters of Sioux City, 1905-06, Vol. 2, pp. 85-102.

STARR, FREDERICK (1897), Summary of the Archaeology of Iowa. Proceedings of the Davenport Academy of Sciences, Vol. 6, pp. 53-124.

VAN HYNING, T. (1910), The Boone Mound. Archaeological Bulletin, Vol. 1, No. 4, pp. 92-94.

VAN VOORHIS, F.L. (n.d.), Mill Creek Pre-historic Indian Culture. Manuscript on file at Sanford Museum, Cherokee.

Western Iowa Prehistory

The People 1

We know something about the cultures that inhabited western Iowa, but we know very little of the people themselves. Were they tall or short? What was the average age at death? What sort of diseases plagued them? What kinds of abnormalities and deficiencies did they have? What of infant mortality? For these questions and many more, there is no single answer. During the last 11,000 years numerous human populations spread across the area we now know as western Iowa and they were far from uniform—either culturally or biologically.

Such diverse factors as climate, technology, diet, genetics, trade and culture history served to determine the kind of cultural and environmental adaptation a given human population would assume. To obtain needed information about the people of the past it is necessary to

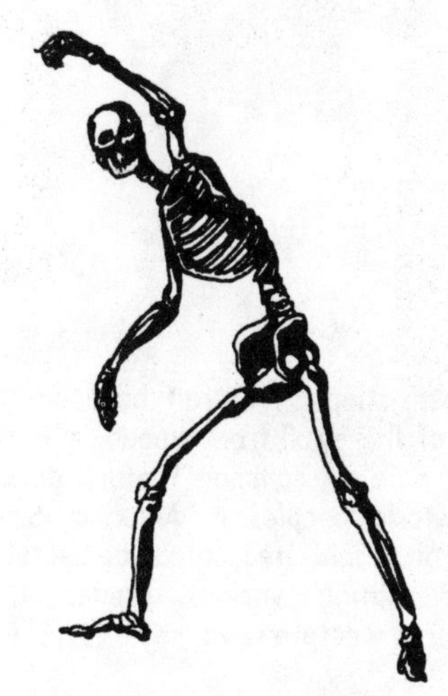

Human bones can provide many insights into the lives of prehistoric peoples. Diseases, injuries, diet, sex, age at death and stature can all be deduced adding another dimension to our knowledge of the past.

examine human bones and associated artifacts from different time periods. This necessitates the careful and respectful excavation of cemetery areas and the detailed analysis of their contents.

No systematic study of human remains has ever been conducted in western Iowa, for two reasons. First, the work done has been almost entirely in the realm of "salvage" when bones have been found during construction, terracing, road building or as a result of vandalism or erosion. Second, a lack of manpower and money exists. Very often remains go unreported and archeologists find out only later that a site has been bulldozed or looted. Even when sites are salvaged and the results made available, they are often inadequate either through lack of sufficient detail or through the fragmentary nature of the remains themselves. Rarely can a skeleton be readily assigned to a particular cultural group.

In spite of this lamentable lack of knowledge a few facts remain that we do know. For example, stature, sex and age at death can be determined in many cases if the remains are complete enough to allow measurement and study. Occasionally it is even possible to speculate on the cause of death. A number of diseases and abnormalities also can be recognized by examination of bones and teeth. Prehistoric man suffered from a variety of infections, tumors and deficiency diseases. If these afflictions can be analyzed we will not only learn a great deal about the

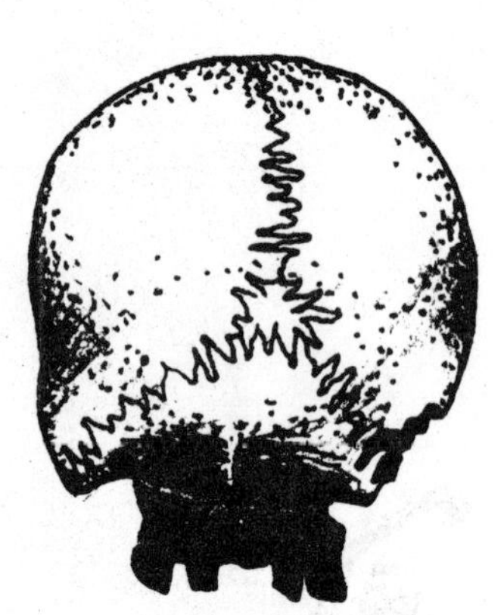

The star-shaped "extra" bone on the back of this skull from Woodbury County is a fairly common feature among prehistoric peoples in America. Since the trait is inherited, it may be useful in differentiating various groups that inhabited western Iowa.

history of specific diseases, but we will be able to better understand the relationship of geographic and environmental factors and draw inferences on the influence of disease on culture. Once these facts are made known and associated with given prehistoric cultures, another dimension is added to our knowledge and understanding of the people of the past.

Even though several isolated skeletons have been studied extensively, it is difficult to apply what is known of a single individual to the group he represents. In order to make meaningful generalizations it is necessary to study a group of skeletons. Only then will it be possible to make statements like "The Oneota were tall," or "The Great Oasis people suffered greatly from tooth decay." Population studies have been made in areas of the southwestern United States and along the Missouri River in South Dakota where entire cemeteries have been excavated. The same kinds of studies have been done in Egypt and places in Europe. But few extensive cemetery areas are known in western Iowa. Therefore, the best approach to the problem is through the excavation and analysis of burials over the entire area. Taken together they will provide a composite picture of the nature of human populations in the past. At the same time much will be learned of mortuary practices and religious beliefs through time. Perhaps it is well to ask: What exactly has been learned? Indeed, it has been argued that researchers can learn nothing from the study of human bones. To

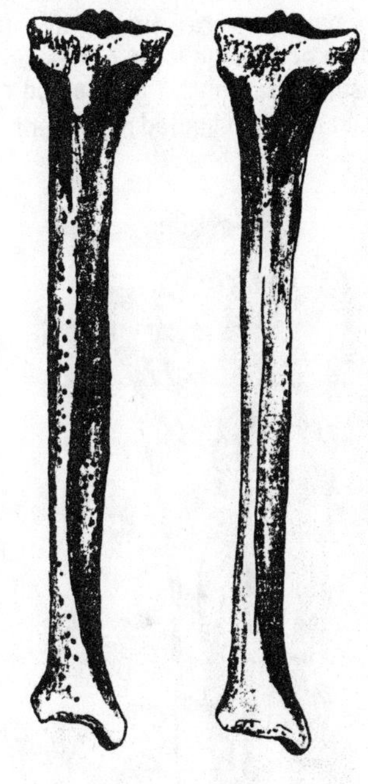

The shinbone at left is from a normal person. The one on the right is porous and lightweight due to demineralization that takes place as a result of old age. This bone was from a partial skeleton salvaged near Correctionville.

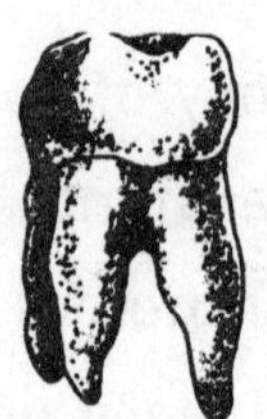

Prehistoric toothaches were common and sometimes very serious. The person whose jaw appears at left had pyorrhea and several large cavities. At right, a normal molar is compared with a a tooth from Cherokee County that displays an abnormal buildup of cementum around the roots — due perhaps to an infection of the gums.

The two elements of the lower leg shown below were fused by the deposition of a rough layer of new bone as a result of an injury. The person experienced pain and limited movement.

refute that argument, some western Iowa examples will be considered.

The man from Correctionville: In 1957 a gravel pit near Correctionville, Iowa, was the scene of a great deal of activity. In the course of the work a large Oneota village and associated burial ground were destroyed. Members of the Northwest Iowa Archeological Society and the Sanford Museum staff worked at the site and managed to salvage some of the material including two human skeletons. One was fairly complete.

Through an examination of the size of the bones and the shape of the pelvis and the eye sockets, the individual was determined to be a male. A study of the lines separating the bones of the skull and the place where the two halves of the pelvis join indicated that he was about 30 years old at the time of death. "Extra" bones were found in two places on the skull and he had an "extra" hole for nerves in two of the backbones of his neck. Both of these traits are inherited and were probably shared to a degree by his relatives. He was troubled with arthritis in his lower back and his teeth were a source of continuing discomfort.

Was he an Oneota man of average health in his day? Do the "inherited traits" appear on his kinsmen? We can only wonder at this stage.

The woman from Anthon: A construction crew working in Anthon, Iowa, in 1960 uncovered the skeleton of an Oneota woman while digging under the city street. The bones were generally in good condition, but there was one unusual feature. A small unnotched triangular arrowhead (like those used by the Oneota) was found imbedded in one of the backbones in such a way that it severed the spinal cord. Although the injury would very likely have had a crippling effect, the woman did not die immediately. Bone began to build up over the arrow point and one of the ribs became fused to the backbone as a result of the injury. It may ultimately have been the cause of death. A study of the woman's pelvis indicated that she was 35-39 years old. Unfortunately, this estimate could not be confirmed through a study of the skull. One of the workmen on the construction project kept it with the idea of making it into a lamp. This incident provides us with an unpleasant example of the need for proper and respectful treatment of all human remains, whether native American, early historic or modern.

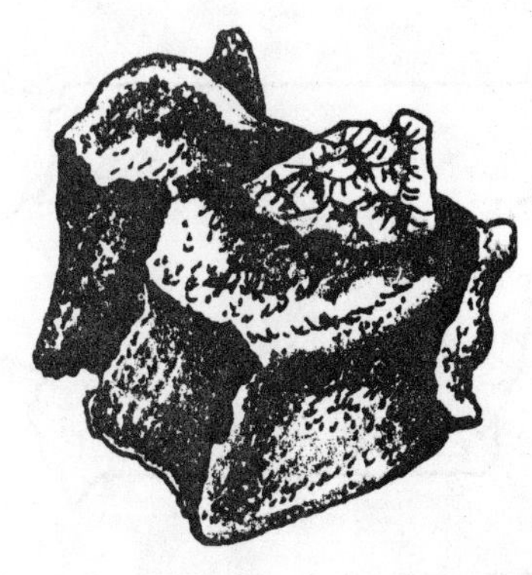

Prehistoric peoples were occasionally shot with arrows. The backbone above and collarbone at lower left were found in a mass grave in Plymouth County.

The bone at lower right is a portion of the leg behind the kneecap. It was found in a Cherokee County mound along with the human effigy pendant pictured in Chapter 3. Although some such injuries may have been accidental, others no doubt attest to feuds among prehistoric peoples.

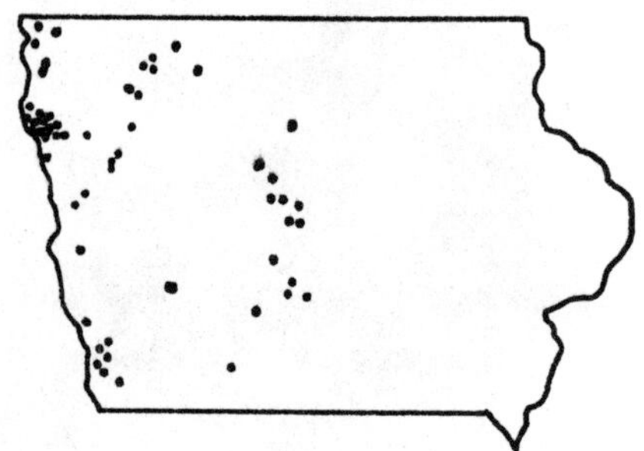

PREHISTORIC BURIAL SITES
IN WESTERN IOWA

Once an Oneota, always an Oneota: If enough material is available it is possible to assign an adult skeleton to a cultural group even if artifacts are not found. When people live together in isolation for a period of time, certain traits are bred into the population. Things like the shape of the head, average height and many subtler differences distinguish peoples. In another case near Sioux City the man, aged 35-45 years, was rather tall — being just over 6 feet. In studying this individual, physical anthropologists measured the skull and compared it with those of several others. They found it to be more like known Oneota skulls than any other. Therefore, they were able to suggest Oneota affiliation even though no artifacts were found. They noted that if a larger sample were available,

This coral gorget was found with a burial eroding from a road cut near Hinton in Plymouth County. It may have been suspended around the neck of the individual. Although the surface is now pitted, it was probably highly polished and very striking at the time of burial.

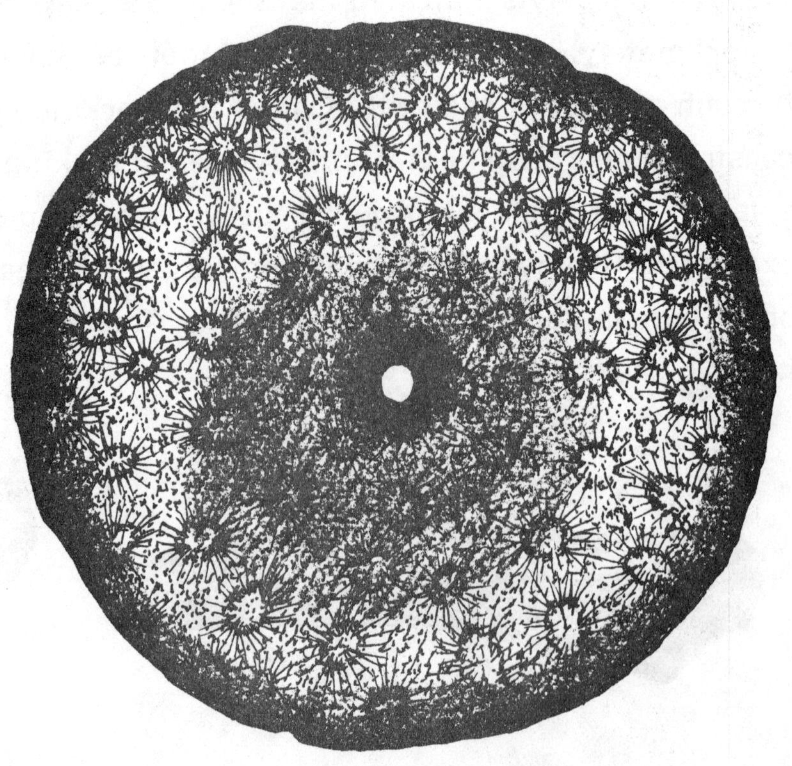

statistical analysis would make it possible to demonstrate racial identity on much firmer grounds.

Dental problems: On a cold January 1, 1955, members of the Northwest Iowa Archeological Society discovered human bones protruding from a bank of Mill Creek. An adult male approximately 35-40 years old was removed in a plaster cast along with two children. All were crowded into a small burial pit. The plaster cast was later excavated. The adult had the worst teeth on record in western Iowa. The roots of his teeth had a lumpy deposit of cementum on them — perhaps the result of pyorrhea. He had painful abscesses around the roots of three teeth and three others were almost completely destroyed by decay. Only black lumps would have protruded above the gum line. Three other teeth had large cavities. This man was pretty healthy otherwise, except for a small amount of arthritis in his lower back. Nothing was found with the bones that would make cultural determination possible. If more material from western Iowa could have been studied, this individual's culture might have been tentatively assigned.

High mortality among the young: After an aboriginal cemetery area had been torn up by looters north of Sioux City, Iowa, the Northwest Iowa Archeological Society was called in to salvage the site. Workers established controls and excavated over 10,000 bone fragments representing at least 27 people. The bones were in no order and all were broken. Undoubtedly the bones had been moved to that

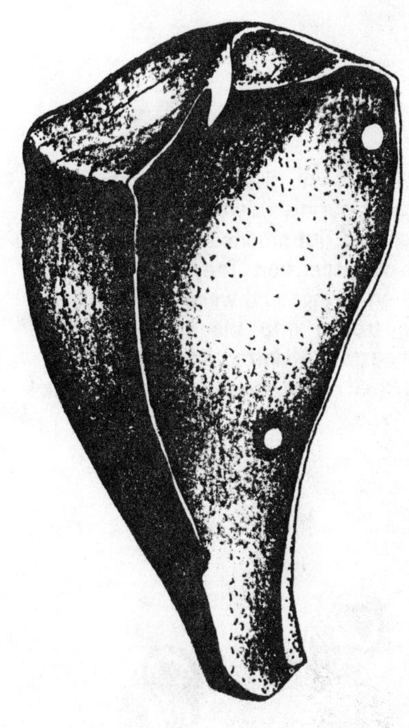

Conch shells were probably symbols of wealth and status among the Great Oasis and Mill Creek peoples. This shell originated in the Gulf of Mexico and was traded into this area. It was found with an adolescent burial in O'Brien County.

Anculosa snail shell beads often accompany burials in western Iowa. They are ground flat on one side to produce a hole or suspension. They were probably worn on strings and were highly prized, being traded into the area from the southeastern United States. Those illustrated here were found in Polk County.

hilltop and reburied during aboriginal times. A detailed study of the bone fragments indicated that more than half the people buried were youngsters including three infants, thirteen children and eleven adults. These figures indicate that mortality among the young was high—as is often the case under aboriginal living conditions.

Trade with northeastern Iowa: A skeleton was rescued from a roadcut near Hinton, Iowa, in 1970. No diagnostic artifacts were found with the burial, although a few elk teeth and some bird bone tubes were recovered along with a beautifully shaped coral gorget with a hole drilled in the middle. Since the gorget was made of an exotic stone, it was sent to the Iowa Geological Survey for identification. As a result, it was learned that the fossil coral occurred in rocks exposed in Floyd, Butler and Cerro Gordo counties in northeastern Iowa. The item was probably traded into western Iowa and may have been a symbol of status.

Too often the archeologist is cast by the general public as a "grave digger" with all the negative connotations of the term. In fact, some segments of the population would like to have studies of human remains discontinued entirely. This is as impossible from a practical point of view, however, as it is undesirable from a scientific point of view. Let us consider the options open, should human remains be found inadvertently.

Bones could be left alone: Or could they? When human remains are found accidentally it is not safe to assume anything about the individual until the bones have been examined and identified. Suppose the bones were those of a missing person or a victim of foul play, or suppose they were those of an early settler in an unmarked grave. We cannot have unidentified human bones lying around on a construction site or in a cornfield. This would be disrespectful to the individual who was buried. Surely the people of the past are entitled to the same treatment as present-day peoples. Perhaps the question is not whether the remains should be studied, but who should do it and to what extent.

Bones could be investigated by the county coroner: This would allow an "autopsy" to be performed, but most county coroners are ill-equipped to study and interpret the remains from a physical, racial and cultural standpoint— whether prehistoric or early historic. It has almost always been necessary for coroners to call in archeologists and physical anthropologists when they have been charged with studying human remains from unmarked graves. A case in point is the first of the Turin discoveries in Monona County. Here a skeleton (now known as the oldest in Iowa, dating 2770 B.C.) was first thought to be a resident who had disappeared some 15 years earlier. The story was covered by Life magazine (September 19, 1955) where the skeleton is shown on the coroner's couch. As it turned out, the bones were taken to the University of Iowa along with subsequent finds to be examined by anthropologists.

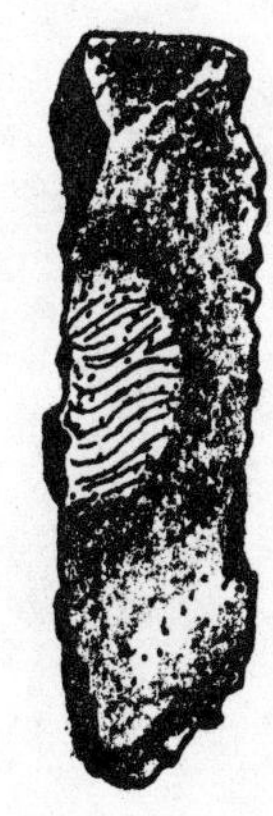

Impressions of fingerprints are occasionally found on bits of pottery. If enough could be found on the floor of a buried house it would be possible to recognize individual women and reconstruct the size of the group and type of social organization.

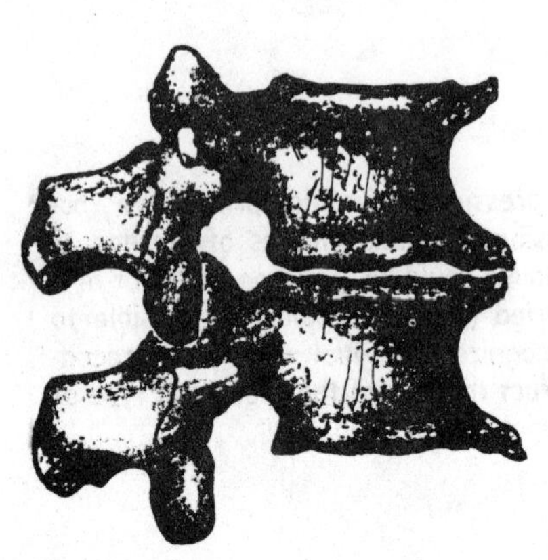

The two vertebrae above came from the lower back of an Oneota man who suffered from a mild case of arthritis. Bony projections extend out linking the backbones causing limited movement and discomfort.

Professional anthropologists could conduct the investigations: When the task of studying unmarked graves is carried out by professional anthropologists, a complete analysis is performed. This includes a description of the circumstances of discovery, an assessment of sex, age at death, stature, diseases, anomalies, racial and cultural identification and any other peculiarities noted. If evidence of foul play with regard to suspected recent interments is noted, the proper authorities can be informed. Such analysis opens the door to proper identification and equal treatment of remains, and enables the information to be integrated into a better understanding of the past. The duty is a solemn one to be performed discreetly by professionals working within the bounds of state laws. The feelings and religious beliefs of any descendants of the deceased must be respected at all times.

It is well to keep this role of the archeologist in its proper perspective. As we shall see in later chapters, archeology consists of much more than unearthing human skeletons.

Sources and Suggested Readings

ANDERSON, DUANE C. (1971), Human Remains in the Sanford Museum Collection. Northwest Iowa Archaeological Society Newsletter, Vol. 19, No. 1, pp. 6-16.

ANDERSON, DUANE C. (1971), The Rubel Burial Site (13PM413). Northwest Iowa Archaeological Society Newsletter, Vol. 19, No. 2, pp. 3-9.

ANDERSON, DUANE C. and DAVID A. BAERREIS (1973), The Rock Creek Ossuarry, Iowa (13PM65).   Proceedings of the Iowa Academy of Science,   Vol. 80, No. 4, pp. 185-191.

BASS, WILLIAM M. (1971), Human Osteology: A Laboratory Manual of the Human Skeleton. Missouri Archaeological Society, Special Publication.

BASS, WILLIAM M. and C.L. BERNEKING (1965), A Possible Oneota Burial found near Sioux City, Iowa. Journal of the Iowa Archeological Society, Vol. 13, pp. 17-23.

BROTHWELL, D.R. (1965), Digging up Bones. British Museum (Natural History). London.

LILLY, DAVID and ROGER BANKS (1965), A Preliminary Description of a Mill Creek Cemetery Near the Broken Kettle Midden Mound. Iowa Archeological Society Newsletter, No. 35, pp. 1-9.

WELLS, CALVIN (1964), Bones, Bodies and Disease, Evidence of Disease and Abnormality in Early Man. Ancient People and Places Series, Vol. 37. Thames and Hudson. London.

Early Hunters

2

The earliest peoples in Iowa were Ice Age hunters. The sketchy picture begins perhaps 12,000 years ago with the Clovis people who hunted extinct mammals such as the mammoth, horse, camel and certain forms of bison. The distinctive features of this early and widespread cultural pattern are the leaf-shaped spear points they manufactured. First recognized in Clovis, New Mexico, Clovis points are now known to be widely distributed. Typically, they have shallow flake scars called "flutes" on either side of the base making them easy to recognize and quite distinctive.

Although the Clovis period is poorly known in Iowa, several sites have been excavated in other states—

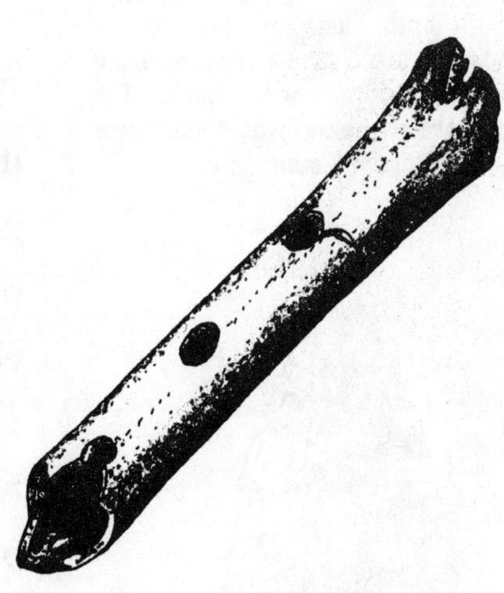

This unique bone whistle was found at the Cherokee Sewer Site in Cherokee County on a level dated 6,000 years old. The item was made from the legbone of a large bird and may have served some religious purpose. It is one of the oldest musical instruments of its kind in North America.

Mammoth hunters used Clovis spear points like the one shown above from Cherokee County. The chip or ''flute'' found on both sides of the base is diagnostic. Later, bison hunters used leaf-shaped Agate Basin points. The example shown below was found near Castana in Monona County.

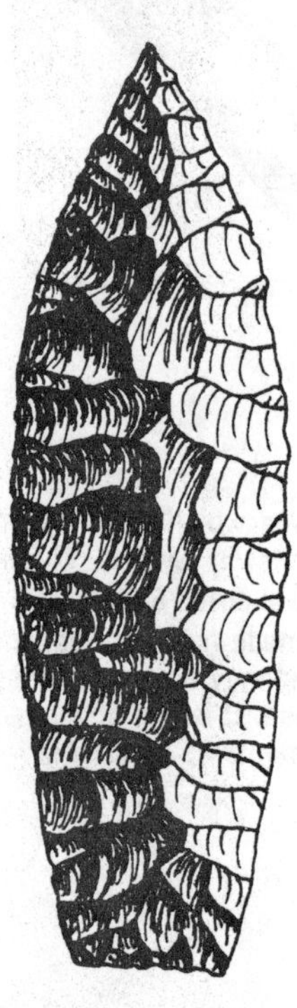

particularly in the West. Iowa finds thus far have either been out of context or from the surface of the ground. A few isolated points have been reported in the western counties raising hopes that a good Clovis site will eventually come to light. One good surface specimen was found on a farm near Pierson some years ago. Another was recovered more recently during the installation of a septic tank near Fort Dodge. Since the state abounds with Ice Age deposits, it seems only a matter of time before we can add a local dimension to the story of the first hunters.

After the disappearance of Clovis peoples, other hunting groups occupied western Iowa prior to 8,500 years ago. Excavations at the Cherokee Sewer Site and surface finds in other western counties indicate that groups of bison hunters continued to use leaf-shaped spear points, but the practice of ''fluting'' was abandoned. Similar cultures were present at the same time across much of the Plains. Like the earlier Clovis peoples, these later groups of hunters appear to have been rather specialized, relying primarily on the herds of game animals for subsistence.

By 8,400 years ago the ''Archaic'' foragers began replacing the earlier cultures. Hunting continued, but a wider range of animals were killed including bison, elk, wolf and coyote. There is evidence that smaller animals and birds were also taken. Spear points in use were triangular in shape and had notches on the side to facilitate tying them onto the shafts of spears. At this time there seems to be a growing reliance on the gathering of wild seeds and other vegetable materials.

Evidence from such early camps as the Hill Site in Mills County shows that stone tools were made and remade using both local rocks and those brought from some distance. Some time before 7,400 years ago these Archaic peoples learned that certain varieties of quartz rocks were made more workable if placed in a fire for a period of time. Once established, this technique was perpetuated into the Historic Period.

An examination of materials from hearths at the Simonsen Site and the Cherokee Sewer Site shows that hackberry seeds were collected, possibly as a seasoning for meat. After a meal it appears to have been common practice to break bones to obtain marrow. In like manner, the brains of large game animals were apparently eaten as evidenced by numerous fractured and scattered skulls. A variety of stone and bone scraping tools have been found on sites indicating that hides were dressed, probably for clothing, containers and perhaps temporary shelter. Bone awls, made from split ribs and longbones are thought to have been used for sewing skins together.

What was life like for these early cultures? Since little direct archeological evidence exists we must base our speculative reconstruction on what is known of living groups of hunters such as the African Bushmen, Australian Aborigines and native hunters of Canada. If

Side-notched spear points were in use by 8,400 years ago in western Iowa. It is likely that a device called a "spear thrower" was in use by this time. It consisted of a wooden handle that acted as an extension of the arm serving to increase the distance and penetration of the spear. The points were probably tied to the shafts with rawhide.

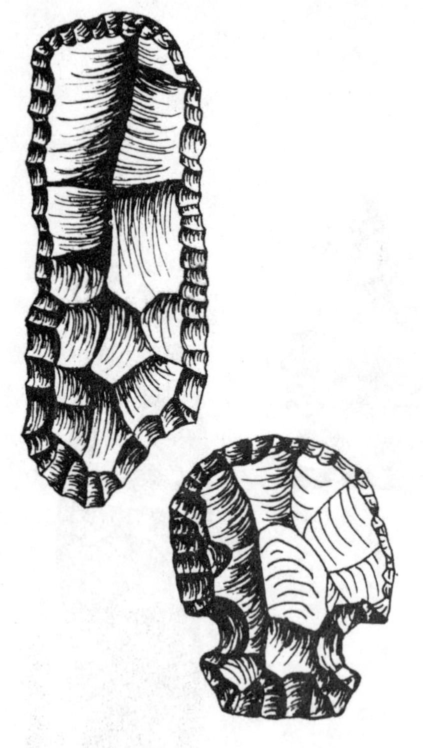

this analogy is justifiable we might expect our Iowa hunters to have been nomadic, ranging over a broad area. Camps probably were occupied for rather short periods of time and housing was temporary. Without the ability to store food they could not have settled down. Constant relocation required the use of only the most meager and portable tools. Their hand-to-mouth economy permitted only low population densities in any given area and regulated how complex their society could become.

Small bands of closely related family groups analogous to those of living hunters probably occupied western Iowa

Hide scrapers were used to remove flesh and hair from hides. Notched forms were common 7,000 years ago on the Prairies. These examples were unearthed in Cherokee County (left) and Mills County (right).

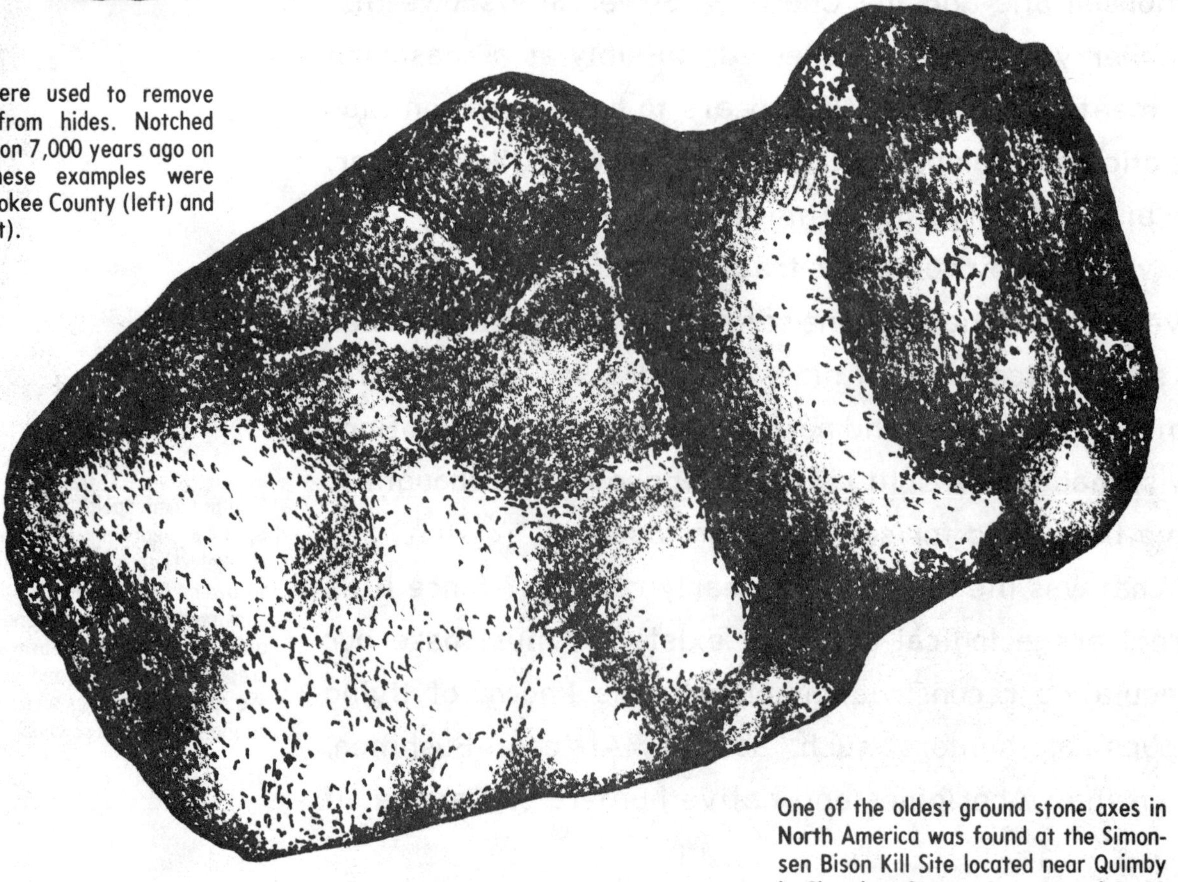

One of the oldest ground stone axes in North America was found at the Simonsen Bison Kill Site located near Quimby in Cherokee County. It was used 8,400 years ago to break up bison carcasses during butchering.

Incised bone is rare on early sites. This example was recovered from the Hill Site in Mills County. Sharp chips of stone called "gravers" were used to cut bone.

from the earliest times. It is likely that each ranged over a fairly well-defined territory that was considered the property of the group. Each probably considered itself to be related through kinship to others in the region. Relationships between groups were probably perpetuated through the exchange of marriage partners, since incest rules would have prohibited marrying a member of one's own band.

Among contemporary primitive hunters, when a couple marries they usually join the man's band. This serves to keep the band strong since males are needed to cooperate in hunting activities. The woman's jobs of gathering food and caring for the children are ones she can do alone. Although her work is every bit as important to the well-being of the family, it does not require the teamwork hunting does.

Early in Iowa's prehistory, related bands probably joined forces and organized communal bison hunts. The extent of two different cultural layers at the Cherokee Sewer Site (larger than a football field) may be indicative of this kind of event. Broken bones, tools and other refuse were found scattered about the camping areas, but only

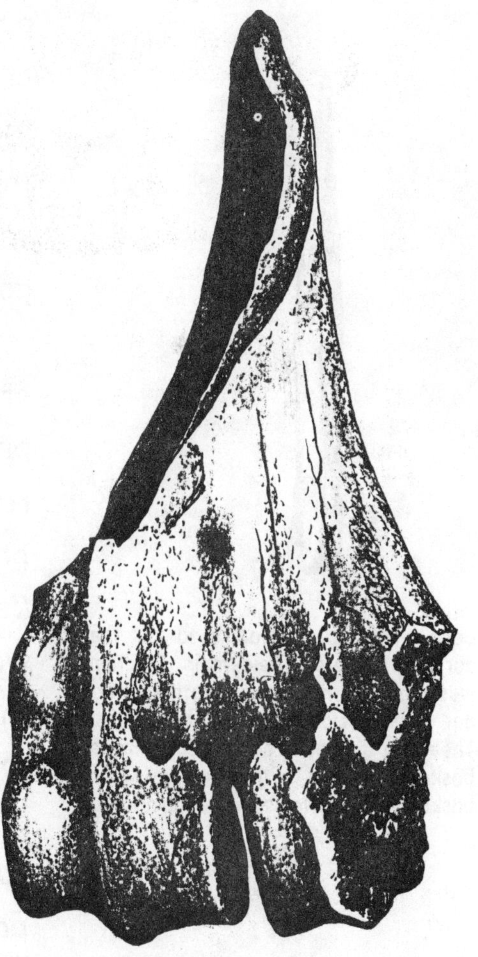

Bone "picks" made from the lower legs of bison were found on the 7,400-year-old level at the Cherokee Sewer Site. They may have been used to get under muscle attachments during the process of butchering bison.

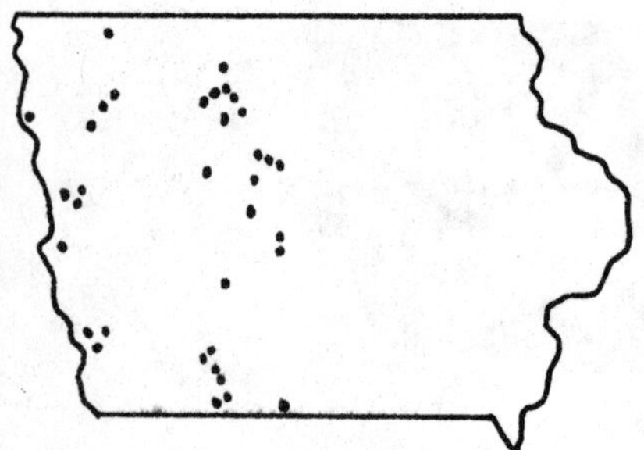

EARLY HUNTER SITES
IN WESTERN IOWA

Bone awls were often used by the earliest hunters. Their main function was probably in punching leather in order to sew clothing and other items. They may also have been used to make basketry, but it is not known when basketry came into use in western Iowa.

the most durable items have survived Iowa's climate. We are left with no information about such perishable items as basketry, bags, string, foot gear or articles of clothing, but it seems safe to assume these things were present.

How did these bands of hunters and gatherers govern themselves? If they were anything like living groups of hunters, no chiefs as such ruled. The headmen were probably natural leaders who gained the respect of others in the band through their ability as hunters or their wisdom in decision making. Such individuals have been demonstrated to be generous and hospitable—to the point of becoming poor themselves. They cooperate with other members of the band working for the good of all in much the same way a father provides for his family in our society. This view is in direct contrast with popularized conceptions portraying a greedy and tyrannical leader.

It is unlikely that there were any specialized institutions or crafts among Iowa's first peoples. Each family probably took care of its own economic, political and religious needs. Certain individuals, usually men, probably served as part-time religious practitioners or "shamans." They were the go-betweens with the spirit world and served as healers or helped to predict the movement of the animal herds or the weather. A marginally sane or even schizophrenic personality is often an asset among primitives in dealing with the supernatural, for spirits are often contacted through possession of the body by the spirit and it "talks" using the body of the shaman. Religious rites such as these often involve dance, chants or music and are usually monotonous, lasting for long periods.

To most primitives, spirits can be good, bad or neutral. In nearly all cases they have to be controlled with magic and ritual. Various taboos are put into effect to check the behavior of the individual not only during the crisis rites (birth, initiation, marriage and death), but during everyday life. The supernaturals dealt with by peoples on this level of development are ones having to do with things the people came into contact with in their environment. Everything (rocks, plants, even wind and lightning) has a spirit.

This "hide grainer" from the Cherokee Sewer Site is made from the ball joint of a bison leg bone. Wear around the margin of this artifact may have resulted from rubbing hides.

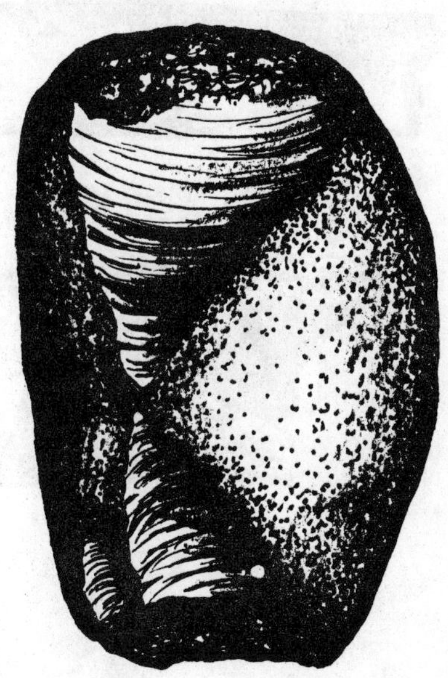

This oblong cobble is spalled and battered on both ends indicating that it served as a hammerstone.

As time passed and man moved farther toward farming as a means of subsistence, religion shifted toward the worship of gods of fertility and ceremonies were directed toward controlling the seasons, the rains and the harvest. Slowly, new elements and ideas were superimposed over those of the earliest cultures. This resulted in population growth and increasingly complex societies.

The fragmentary bison bones illustrated below bear cut marks resulting from butchering. If enough bones can be recovered from a kill site, specific butchering practices can be studied.

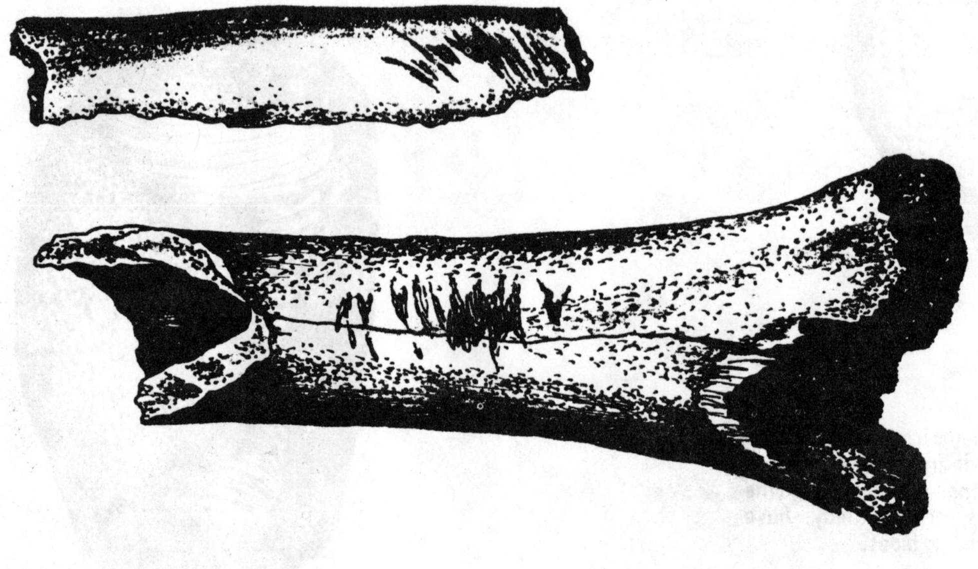

Sources and Suggested Readings

FRANKFORTER, W.D. (1959), A Pre-ceramic Site in Western Iowa. Journal of the Iowa Archeological Society, Vol. 8, No. 4, pp. 47-72.

FRANKFORTER, W.D. and GEORGE A. AGOGINO (1960), The Simonsen Site: Report for the Summer of 1959. Plains Anthropologist, Vol. 5, No. 10, pp. 65-70.

REEVES, BRIAN (1973), The Concept of an Altithermal Cultural Hiatus in Northern Plains Prehistory. American Anthropologist, Vol. 75, No. 5, pp. 1221-1253.

SERVICE, ELMAN R. (1966), The Hunters. Prentice-Hall, Inc. Englewood Cliffs, N.J.

SHUTLER, RICHARD, DUANE C. ANDERSON, et al. (1974), Preliminary Report of a Stratified Paleo-Indian/Archaic Site in Northwestern Iowa. Journal of the Iowa Archeological Society, IN PRESS.

WILMSEN, EDWIN N. (1965), An Outline of Early Man Studies In The United States. American Antiquity, Vol. 31, No. 1, pp. 172-192.

WORMINGTON, H.M. (1957), Ancient Man in North America. Denver Museum of Natural History, Popular Series No. 4.

First Potters 3

The Woodland culture is the most widely distributed in western Iowa and one of the most poorly known. Best guesses place the beginning of this culture pattern in the western counties around the time of Christ. Woodland groups occupied the area for about 1,000 years and ultimately blended with other groups in the Late Prehistoric Period. The two main distinguishing features of Woodland culture are thick, cord-marked pottery and low, rounded burial mounds.

Woodland culture had its origin in the Eastern Woodlands of the United States as early as 1000 B.C. By 300 B.C., a distinctive pattern called "Hopewell" appeared. As time passed, this culture spread westward to the prairies and then across the plains to the base of the Rocky Mountains. Hopewellian artifacts found in the eastern heartlands of the Ohio and Illinois River valleys are quite elaborate. Sites often demonstrate extensive planning, mounds, earthen enclosures, moats and fortifications indicating a fairly large population and a good deal of social control by a priestly class. In eastern Iowa

Two views of an amulet made of red pipestone found in a mound near Cherokee. It is one of the few carvings of a human form known in western Iowa. The back side depicts a stylized bison shot with an arrow.

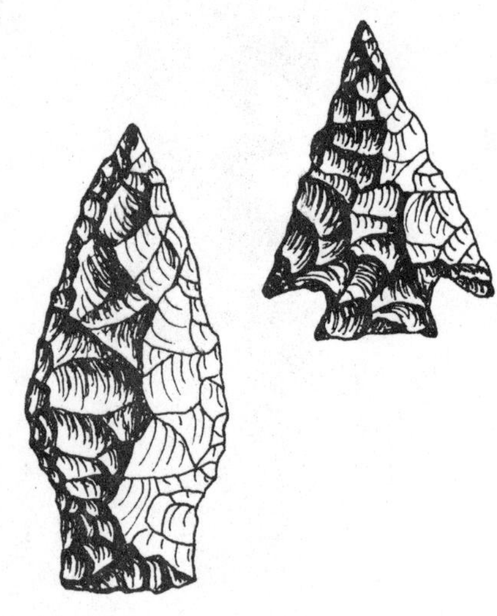

Woodland spear points are commonly "stemmed" or corner notched as shown above. The point below with its broad blade and ovoid shape is more typically found in Hopewellian Woodland sites in eastern Iowa. This specimen was found along the Des Moines River.

and southwestern Wisconsin the "effigy mounds" were constructed by later Woodland peoples who had contemporaries in western Iowa.

In the western counties of the state, Woodland culture was considerably more simple, lacking the elaborate artifacts and earthworks of eastern Iowa. Some repetition of the prevailing Woodland theme involved the so-called "burial cult." Considerable time and energy went into the construction of burial mounds which were generally a few feet high and 20-40 feet across. Many of the sites known contain groups of these mounds in clusters of from two to six. A typical mound might contain a variety of items including human bones or bone fragments, cremations, burial offerings and perhaps some items of everyday life.

The mounds may have been ceremonial centers used by people living over a wide area. At times they appear to be associated with larger camps or villages. Some mounds appear to have been built up by successive burials which gradually enlarged the mounds over a long period of time. Still others seem to contain a central important individual often extended on his back and surrounded by cremations or flexed burials—perhaps representing sacrificial victims or servants ritually killed at the time of burial of the central figure. Very often Woodland mounds contain little that can be dated and occasionally artifacts are totally lacking, making interpretation difficult.

It appears that by a conscious effort on the part of the Woodland peoples, burial areas were made into per-

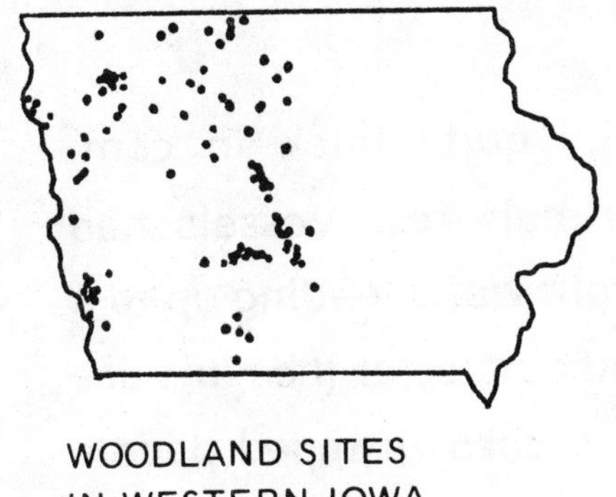

WOODLAND SITES
IN WESTERN IOWA

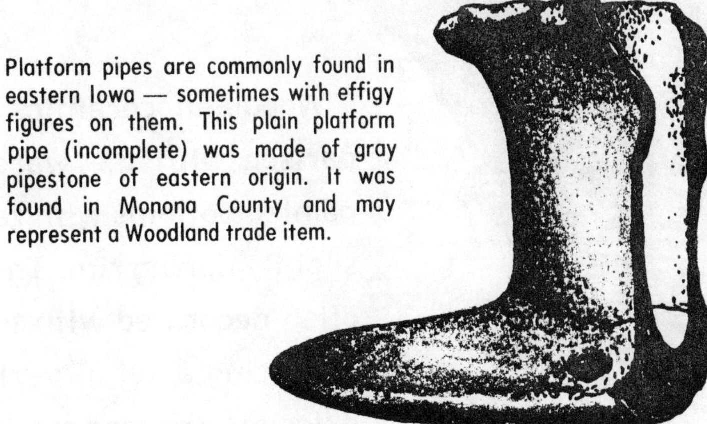

Platform pipes are commonly found in eastern Iowa — sometimes with effigy figures on them. This plain platform pipe (incomplete) was made of gray pipestone of eastern origin. It was found in Monona County and may represent a Woodland trade item.

manent and enduring monuments—a practice related to the more impressive earthworks of the eastern United States. Not all Woodland sites are burial mounds. Camp sites have been recognized although little work has been done on this aspect of western Iowa prehistory. No houses or villages have been definitely recorded although they may have existed. No corn or other agricultural crop has yet been reported from western Iowa, but it is quite likely that certain crops were cultivated. Corn, for example, is known from Woodland sites in South Dakota and eastern Iowa.

Marshy conditions which ruled out farming probably persisted throughout Woodland times and perhaps beyond. Perhaps such other resources as small game, fish, waterfowl, wild rice and other native plants provided the basis for subsistence on a hunting and gathering level of development. If so, groups were settled enough, even if they were small, to base their activities around a ceremonial center and to make use of pottery that often was bulky and difficult to transport.

"Adena" spear points are rare in western Iowa. They may represent Early Woodland occupation of the area. The diagnostic feature is the rounded stem at the base. This specimen was found near the Big Sioux River in Plymouth County.

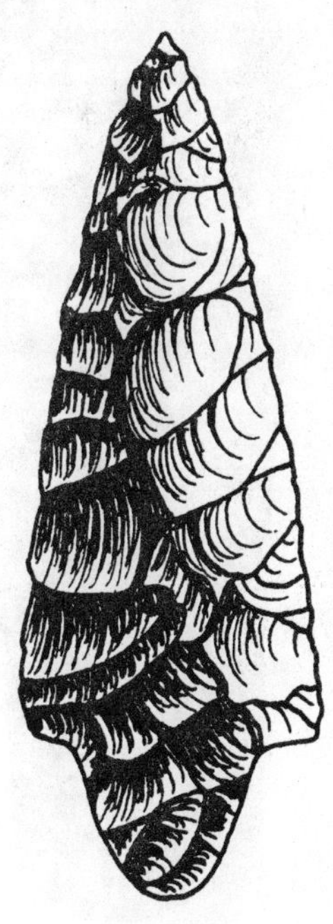

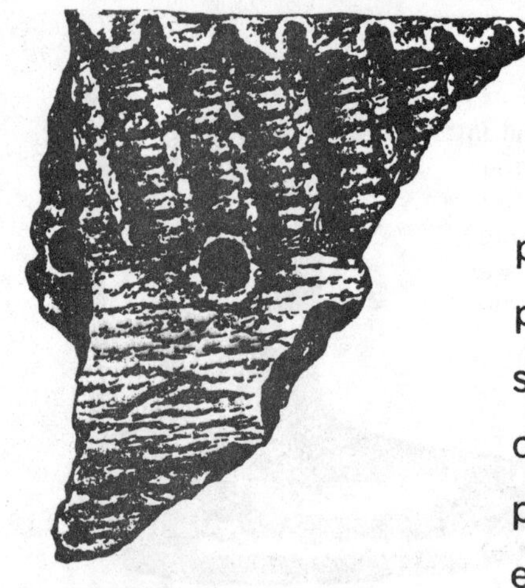

Cord wrapped paddles like the reconstruction below were used to shape pottery vessels by slapping the moist clay over an anvil stone. This produced a cord marked surface as shown above. The paddle was turned on edge and pressed into the rim of the vessel to produce diagonal lines. Decorative holes were pressed into the rim with a bone tool or stick. The specimen above was found near Fort Dodge.

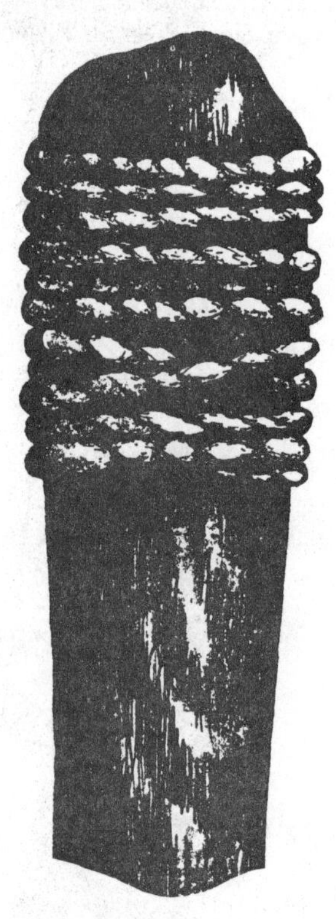

Woodland ceramics are usually quite thick in comparison with the wares of later cultures. Vessels had pointed bottoms with rather straight walls leading up to a slightly flaring rim. The inside and outside of the rims are often decorated with the edge of a cord-wrapped paddle producing a set of vertical or diagonal depressions. The exteriors are cord marked by slapping the moist clay with the flat side of the paddle. Rounded bumps or "bosses" often ornament the neck of the pot. They are produced by pressing a stick through the moist clay from within.

Woodland pottery offers a unique opportunity to study the cordage and weaving used by the Woodland peoples. Very often patterns are imprinted in the clay with sufficient detail to learn how the plant fibers were twisted and braided. Some vessels were decorated with fabric by pressing a woven design into the moist clay. This makes it possible to study the weaving techniques known to these peoples. We assume that even the earliest cultures used some forms of woven bags or containers, but it is not often that evidence of these perishable items is preserved.

The classic "Hopewellian" Woodland cultures of the East typically have rather large quantities of trade items included with their burial mounds. In Ohio and Illinois, Great Lakes copper is found along with exotic stone from the South, bear teeth from the Rocky Mountains and seashells from the Gulf of Mexico. In western Iowa, Woodland peoples were not as well blessed, although Gulf shell beads and exotic stone items did find their way into the area indicating that trade routes were open.

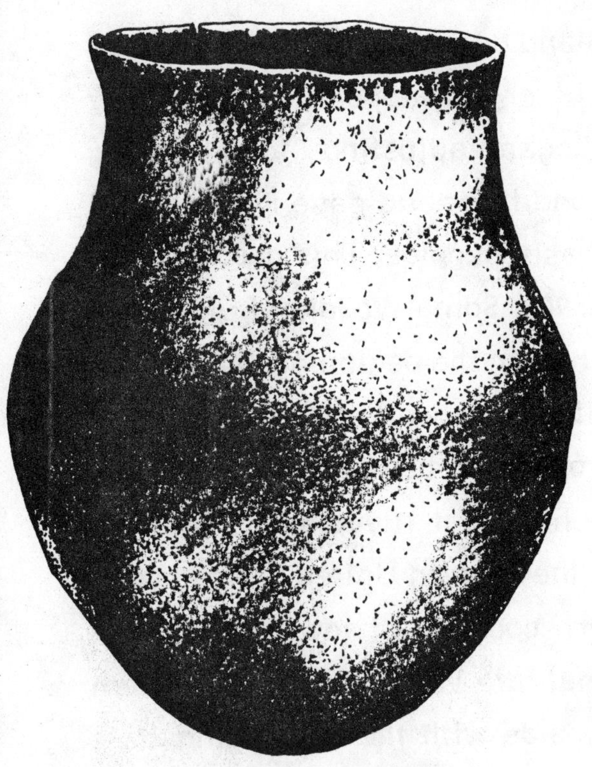

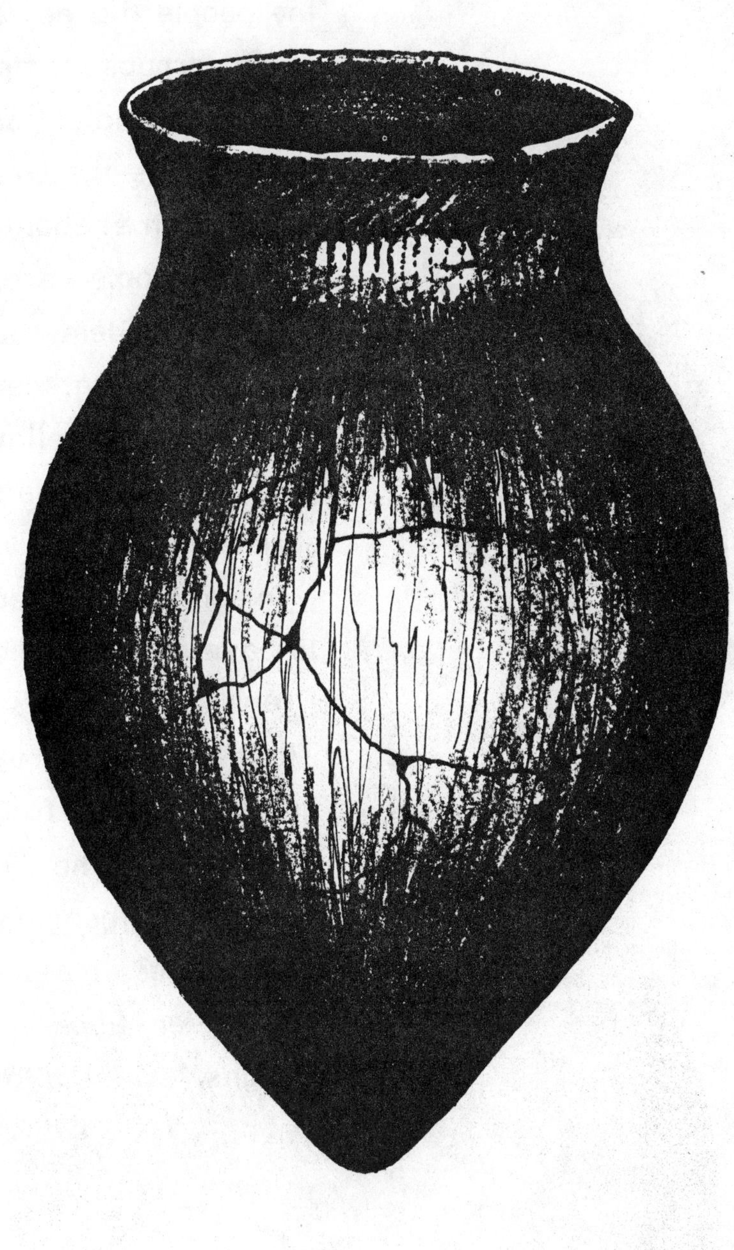

The "Sterns Creek" Woodland peoples who lived along the Missouri River made plain rounded pots (above), while more typical pointed bottom vessels were made by Hopewellian Woodland peoples elsewhere in western Iowa. The three-quarter grooved axe (below) was widely used by Woodland peoples. (Pottery shown one-third size; axe shown one-half size.)

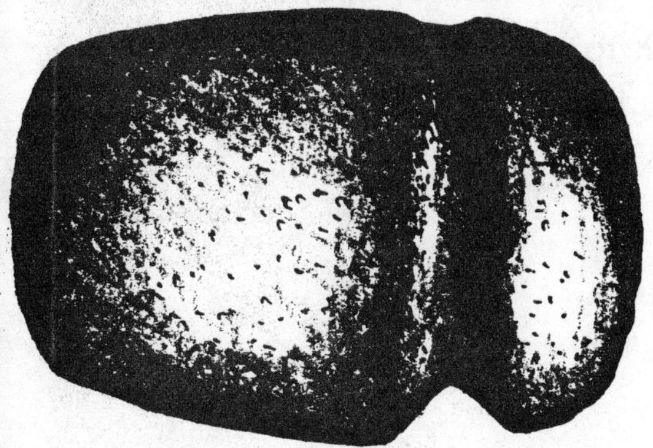

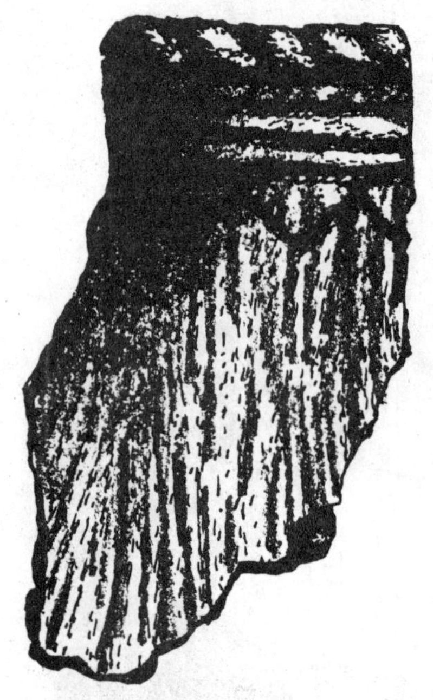

The ''Missouri Bluffs'' Woodland peoples represent another departure from Hopewellian groups. Pottery was decorated with a paddle, but string was pressed into the clay around the rim to produce horizontal lines and triangles. This culture has been recognized in several of the extreme western counties.

At the close of the Woodland occupation of western Iowa the people did not die out or ''disappear.'' Apparently some groups simply began adjusting to changing ecological and cultural conditions and gave rise to what we know as the Great Oasis peoples. This process may have begun at about A.D. 900. Some Woodland ideas and perhaps people were involved in the beginnings of the Mill Creek and Glenwood cultures as well. New methods of pottery making, new crops and new forms of social, political and religious life that developed first in Mesoamerica and later in the eastern United States began spreading into the western counties of Iowa.

In some areas traditional late Woodland peoples seem to have persisted side by side with the developing Late Prehistoric cultures discussed in the next few chapters. The Woodland survivals probably continued to occupy areas unsuitable for farming for perhaps as much as 200 years after the more settled village peoples had established themselves and for a time they were contemporaries. In at least one site in Emmet County, Woodland potters apparently tried to copy Mill Creek ceramic designs, testifying to the influence of their new neighbors.

Sources and Suggested Readings

ANDERSON, DUANE C. (1970), The Catlinite Amulet Site (13CK64). Iowa Archeological Society Newsletter, No. 56, pp. 2-13.

CHRISTENSEN, THOMAS P. (1952), The Mound Builders. Annals of Iowa, Vol. 31, pp. 300-308.

FLANDERS, RICHARD E. and REX HANSMAN (1961), A Woodland Mound Complex in Webster County, Iowa. Journal of the Iowa Archeological Society, Vol. 11, No. 1, pp. 1-12.

HEROLD, ELAINE BLUHM (1970), Hopewell: Burial Mound Builders. Palimpsest, Vol. 51, No. 12, pp. 497-528.

McKUSICK, MARSHALL (1964), Prehistoric Man in Northeastern Iowa. Palimpsest, Vol. 45, No. 12, pp. 465-494.

McKUSICK, MARSHALL (1970), The Davenport Conspiracy. Office of the State Archaeologist, Report No. 1.

ORR, ELLISON (1963), Iowa Archaeological Reports 1934-1939 (ten volumes) with an Evaluation and Index by Marshall McKusick. Archives of Archaeology, No. 20.

VAN HYNING, T. (1910), The Boone Mound. Records of the Past, Vol. 9, pp. 157-162.

WARD, DUREN J.H. (1905), The Investigation of the Okoboji Mounds and the Finds. Iowa Journal of History and Politics, Vol. 5, No. 3, pp. 8-16.

Conservative Great Oasis

4

In Murray County, Minnesota, a now extinct lake was formed during the Ice Age. It is called Lake Great Oasis and is now entirely dry, but in prehistoric times a village was located along its shoreline. The people who lived there vanished from the area more than 600 years ago. They were first studied in the early 1940's and have since come to be called "the Great Oasis" people. Their pottery decorations so closely resembled the neighboring Mill Creek people in Iowa that the culture was not recognized in this state until about 20 years later. Now the distribution of Great Oasis is known to be quite extensive with sites ranging from Mobridge, South Dakota, to Des Moines, Iowa, and from southwestern Minnesota to northeastern Nebraska.

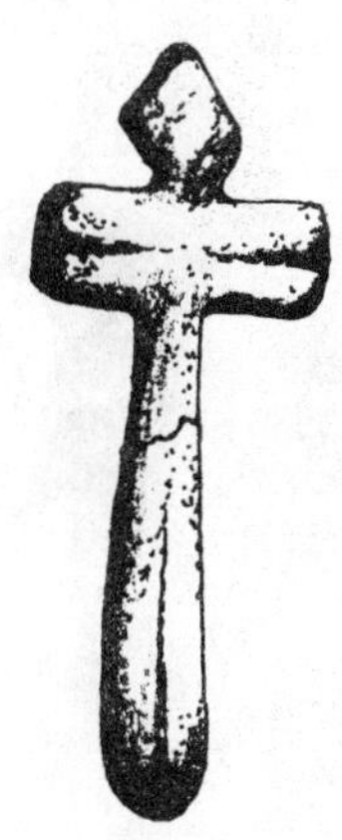

Several "crosses" were found in a cemetery site in West Des Moines in 1963 in association with Great Oasis pottery. The "crosses" predate European contact by a few hundred years and therefore cannot be attributed to Christian origin.

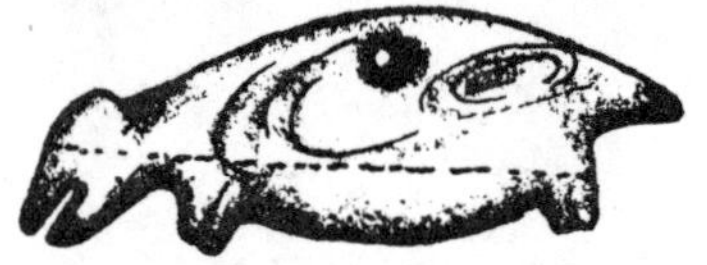

Animal effigies made of red pipestone have been found on Great Oasis and Mill Creek sites. Although their function is not known, they may have been some form of clan symbols.

With the introduction of the bow in western Iowa, projectile points became noticeably smaller. These Great Oasis points from Plymouth County show the typical side-notched form. Long, chipped-stone knives and snubnosed hide scrapers were commonly used by Great Oasis peoples.

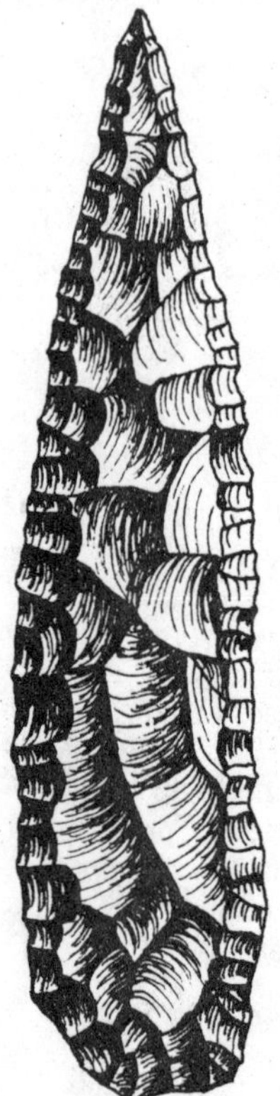

The Great Oasis people seem to be direct descendants of the Woodland peoples who occupied the entire area previously. Drawing on their Woodland ancestry, the Great Oasis peoples were to be conservative (that is, adhering to traditional styles) throughout one of Iowa's most interesting periods—the Late Prehistoric. During this time, A.D. 900-1300, the Great Oasis culture was contemporaneous with three other cultures in western Iowa: Glenwood, Mill Creek and Oneota. So far as is known, they lived in open, unprotected villages composed of several rectangular lodges. Four such structures have been excavated in a village a few miles north of Sioux City. A typical house was about 25 by 40 feet, probably large enough to contain an extended family consisting of parents, grandparents, offspring and perhaps other close relatives. Each lodge was built in a shallow pit about 1½ feet deep with walls of vertical posts interwoven with sticks and plastered with mud.

The roof was probably grass thatch over poles in the shape of a rounded dome over the rectangular structure. All excavated houses also had a covered external entrance. Inside, a typical house had a central fireplace, an ash pit and several storage pits called "cache pits." The latter were used for storage of a variety of household items including food, but were eventually converted into convenient wastebaskets when they became sour. The same kinds of pits were found outside the dwellings as well.

The contents of these storage pits tell much about the habits and diet of the Great Oasis people. Let us draw on the information gathered from the excavation of a single house in Plymouth County. There, remains of deer, elk and bison were found along with wolf, beaver, gopher, rabbit, muskrat, mole, mouse and coyote. Other animals found included twenty-six kinds of birds—waterbirds, birds of prey and perching birds as well as a dozen varieties of fish. The charred remains of corn and sunflower seeds represented cultivated crops while seven other kinds of seeds appear to have been collected for use. Historic Indians are known to have collected plants for such things as food, seasoning, medicine and paint and it is likely that these prehistoric people did the same.

Taken together, the animal remains recovered from this house would have been sufficient to feed a family of six for nearly one year. Deer and elk were the most important source of protein. It has been calculated that more than 5,000 pounds of the 6,300 pounds of meat represented by bones found inside the house was derived from these animals. Other sources of food included clams, frogs, turtles and perhaps even snakes.

Abraders were made from coarse rocks for use in fashioning stone, bone and wooden tools (note grooves). Porous rocks called "klinkers" were often used by western Iowa peoples for this purpose. They originated in the burning lignite beds in the Dakotas and floated down the river to Iowa where they were collected and distributed.

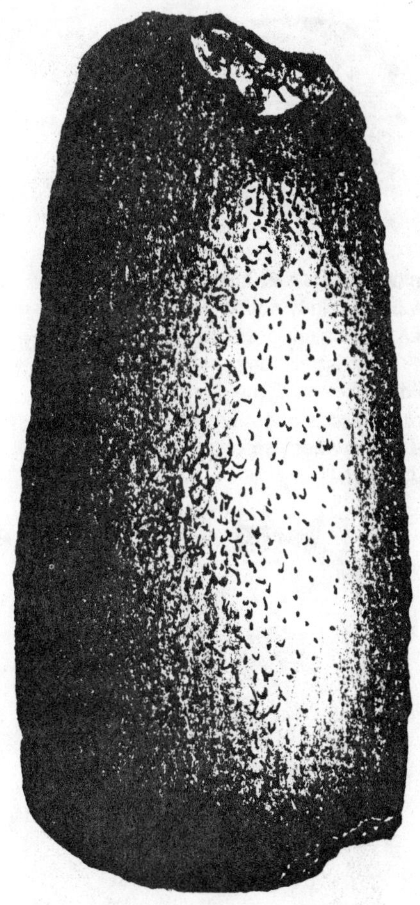

The polished stone celt replaced the three-quarter grooved axe as the principal woodworking tool during the Late Prehistoric Period. Unlike the axe, the blade of the celt is hafted at right angles to the handle.

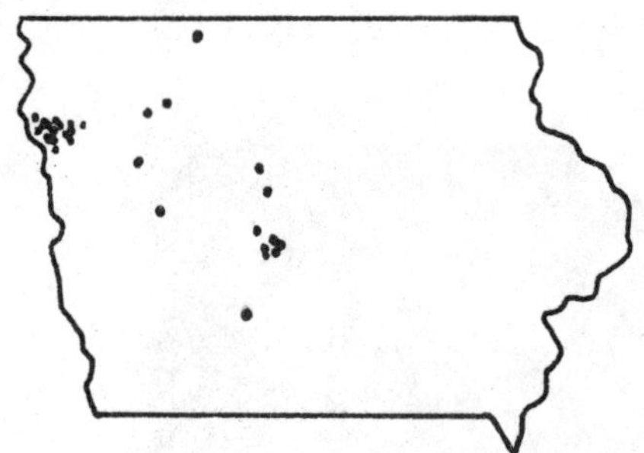

Miniature pots and large ceramic beads are occasionally found on Great Oasis sites. The small pots are also known to the Mill Creek and may have been children's toys. The function of the ceramic beads is not known. Ornaments and even net sinkers have been suggested.

It is obvious these people were exploiting many aspects of their environment. It seems very likely that in addition to domestic tasks the women were occupied with farming activities. The digging stick and perhaps the hoe made with a bison shoulder blade were the main farming implements in use. Garden plots were probably less than an acre on the average and must have required constant attention. Further, it may have been necessary to relocate the plots every few years due to declining fertility. A considerable amount of time and energy must have been expended in felling trees, clearing and burning off brush on new acreage. In this pursuit help may have been solicited from other family groups.

Men were more likely involved with hunting activities, using the bow and arrow which replaced the spear used by earlier cultures. Arrow points and other chipped stone tools used by Great Oasis people were often made from "Nehawka Flint," a durable gray stone bearing tiny fossils. Since it does not occur in northwestern Iowa, this material was probably traded up river from its source in southwestern Iowa or southeastern Nebraska.

It is likely that the main villages of the Great Oasis were largely abandoned during the summer season. Winter occupation is documented at the Plymouth County site by a deer skull with antlers shed; late spring or early summer use of the site is suggested by the discovery of a certain bird bone (the medullary) present only during the reproductive period. Fall presence is indicated by a study of the growth rings on the scales of certain fish. Actually, rather substantial occupation is indicated in the spring and fall by the large number of migratory birds.

What does this indicate about the yearly cycle? Where were these people during the summer season? Two possibilities have been suggested: they may have held communal bison hunts, or perhaps family groups spread up the tributaries to establish small garden plots. Although both ideas may be correct, the latter has some support at the Williams Site in Plymouth County where corn and broken pottery have been found in association

A small fragment of basketry about the size of a dime was found at the Williams Site in Plymouth County. Microscopic examination revealed a kind of weave called "plaiting" pictured above (greatly enlarged).

The commonest variety of Great Oasis pottery features a slightly flaring rim and cord-marked body. Triangular designs or the "stick deer" motif are often found on the exterior of the rim. No handles or effigies are present. A second type of pottery called the "wedge lip form" is equally abundant in certain areas. (Shown about one-third size.)

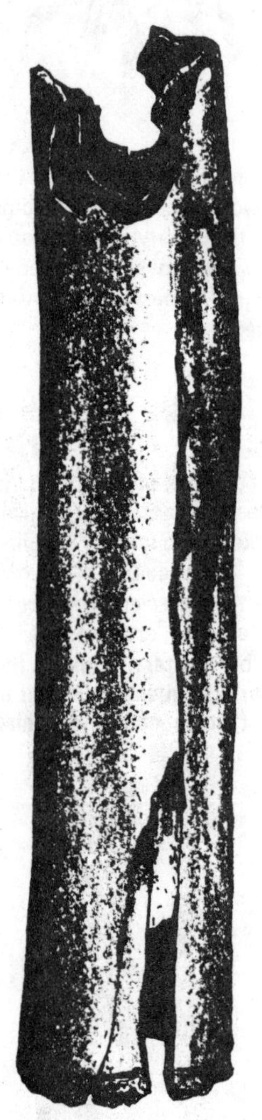

"Bone wrenches" were used as arrow shaft straighteners — probably in conjunction with a heating process. This item (missing upper end and part of drilled hole) was made from the shinbone of a deer.

with a small area of occupation thought to have contained a temporary structure.

In spite of their wide distribution covering parts of four states, the Great Oasis people were not overly influenced by ideas from outsiders. Their Mill Creek neighbors in northwestern Iowa had a much greater variety of pottery styles and a richer artifact inventory but few traits were accepted by the Great Oasis. They did trade with the Mill Creek peoples, thus insuring friendly relations and close contact, yet they retained the conservative nature of their culture until its disappearance from the prehistoric record about A.D. 1300.

For some time archeologists speculated about the placement of the Great Oasis and Mill Creek cultures in time. Judging from the Woodland-like characteristics retained on pottery and rather sparse artifact inventories, some preferred to think of Great Oasis as "early" and ancestral to Mill Creek. Now there is sufficient evidence to warrant the conclusion that the two groups were contemporaries, although Mill Creek may have persisted somewhat longer. It was difficult to accept the idea that one culture does not necessarily become like its neighbor as a result of prolonged contact.

Interaction between the Great Oasis and Mill Creek cultures is seemingly documented at one site in Plymouth County where an abundance of trade items (including Gulf shell, snail-shell beads from the southeastern United States and exotic stone) have been found along with the pottery of both the Great Oasis and Mill Creek cultures. Further, most Great Oasis sites that have been radiocarbon-dated fall well within the Mill Creek time span. The two groups must, therefore, be considered contemporaries. They lived side by side, each adapted to its own natural and cultural environment. If we knew more about the physical details of the skeletons of these populations we might find still more differences between them. It is conceivable that some light might even be shed on the origins of the cultures and aid in the overall interpretation.

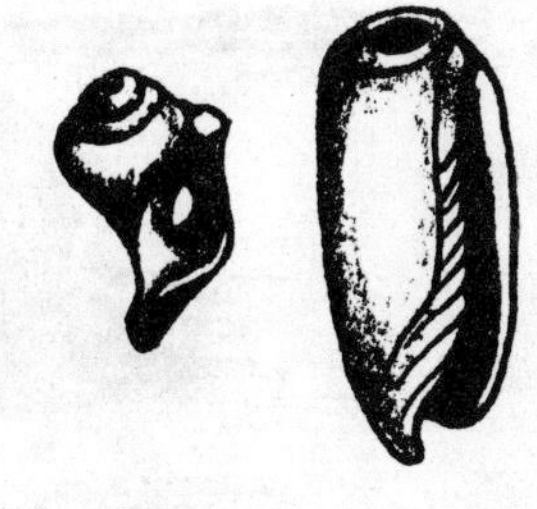

Conch and olive shells from the Gulf of Mexico appear on Great Oasis sites as trade items. They were often drilled and were probably worn as ornaments or status symbols. Tubular and disc shell beads of marine origin were used in the same way.

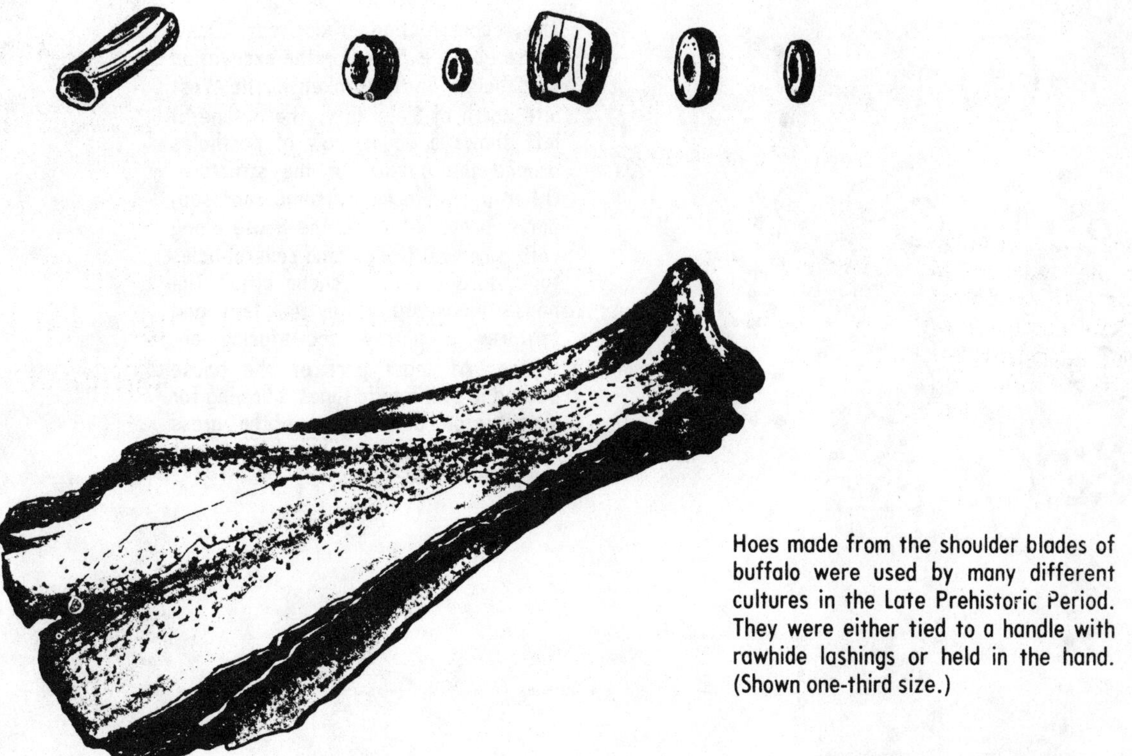

Hoes made from the shoulder blades of buffalo were used by many different cultures in the Late Prehistoric Period. They were either tied to a handle with rawhide lashings or held in the hand. (Shown one-third size.)

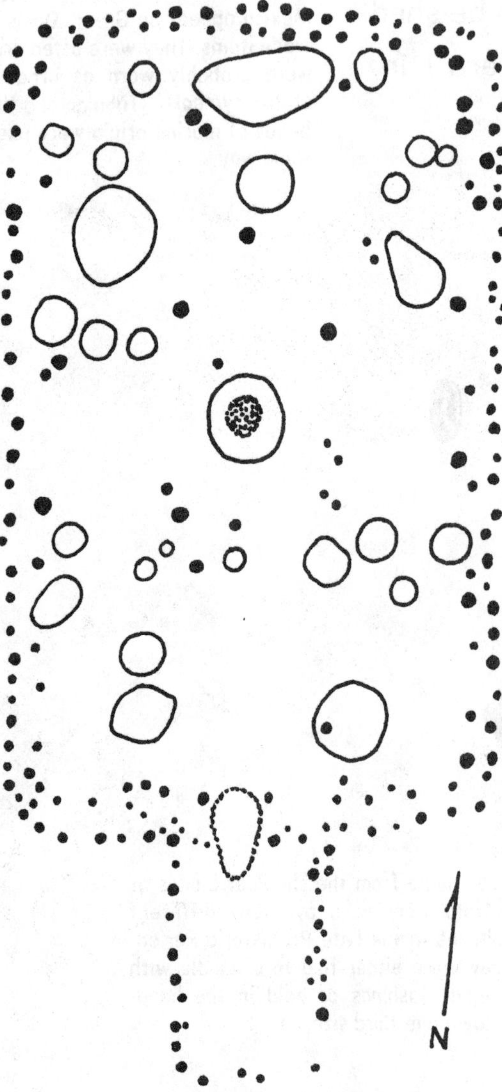

The reconstruction of a Great Oasis house above is based on the excavation of a house at the Broken Kettle West Site north of Sioux City. The outline at left shows a double row of postholes around the outside of the structure. Other posts, including some roof supports, are seen inside the house along with a central fire pit and several holes for storage called "cache pits." The house measured 25 by 40 feet and featured a narrow south-facing entrance. At least part of the house burned in prehistoric times, allowing for preservaton of portions of the grass thatch roof which was found lying over the hard packed floor.

Sources and Suggested Readings

BAERREIS, DAVID A., Ed. (1970), Environmental Archaeology in Western Iowa. Northwest Iowa Archaeological Society Newsletter, Vol. 18, No. 5, pp. 3-15.

HENNING, DALE R. (1967), Mississippian Influences on the Eastern Plains Border: An Evaluation. Plains Anthropologist, Vol. 12, No. 36, pp. 184-194.

HENNING, DALE R. (1971), Great Oasis Culture Distributions. In Prehistoric Investigations, Marshall McKusick (ed.), Office of the State Archaeologist, Report No. 3, pp. 125-133.

JOHNSON, ELDEN (1969), Decorative Motifs on Great Oasis Pottery. Plains Anthropologist, Vol. 14, No. 46, pp. 272-276.

JOHNSTON, RICHARD B. (1967), The Hitchell Site. Publications in Salvage Archeology, No. 3, River Basin Surveys, Smithsonian Institution.

KNAUTH, OTTO (1963), Mystery of the Crosses. Annals of Iowa, Vol. 37, No. 2, pp. 81-91.

WILFORD, LLOYD A. (n.d.), The Great Oasis Village Site. Xerox manuscript, Sanford Museum, Cherokee.

WILFORD, LLOYD A. (n.d.), The Low Village Site, 1950. Xerox manuscript, Sanford Museum, Cherokee.

WILFORD, LLOYD A. (1945), Three Villages of the Mississippian Pattern in Minnesota. American Antiquity, Vol. 11, No. 1, pp. 32-40.

WILLIAMS, PATRICIA M. (1974), The Williams Site (13PM50): A Great Oasis Component in Northwest Iowa. Journal of the Iowa Archeological Society, IN PRESS.

Glenwood at Peace

5

As early as A.D. 900 a new and distinctive pattern of culture was being established in southwestern Iowa and southeastern Nebraska. These people, like the Mill Creek peoples of northwestern Iowa, had a complex of traits, including a variety of pottery shapes with handles and effigies, that link them to Mississippian cultures to the south and east.

The Glenwood peoples, so named because of their proximity to the town bearing that name, built square houses with rounded corners usually measuring about 30 feet on the side. They were constructed in shallow pits with four main roof supports near the middle of the house around the central fire pit. Storage pits were dug into the

Arrow points from the Glenwood area vary little from those made by the Great Oasis and Mill Creek peoples. Often Glenwood points are better made reflecting the availability of good workable stone. Some have two sets of notches on the sides while others are unnotched.

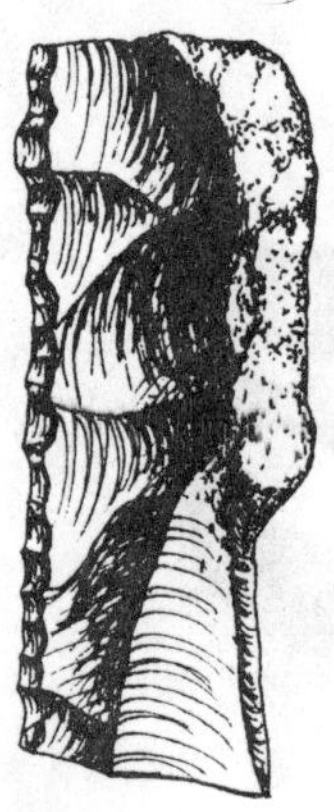

Often, "waste flakes" are used as cutting tools. The flake above was modified by removing small chips from the left margin. The large knife below is finely chipped on both sides. Tools such as these were probably used for skinning animals and cutting meat and other materials.

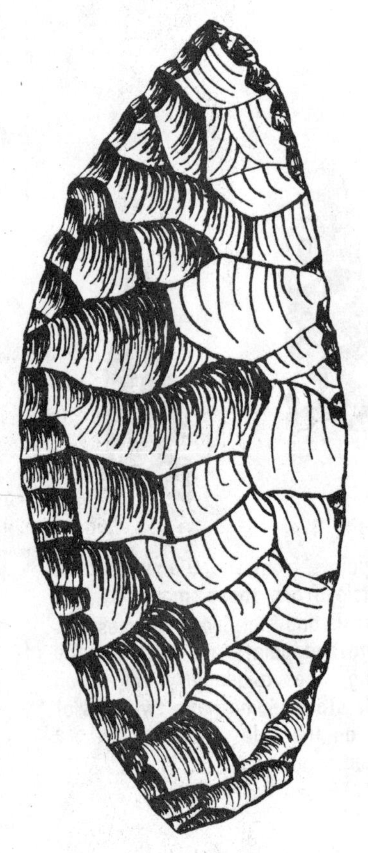

floor of the house. The walls were made of closely set vertical poles. A narrow, covered entrance usually extended from the south wall of the lodge. These structures probably had sod roofs although specific aspects of construction have not been reported in detail. Some houses appear to be isolated along valleys or bluffs overlooking rivers and streams. Other sites feature small clusters of lodges housing a community of perhaps forty to sixty people.

The economy of the Glenwood people was based on the widely accepted crops—corn, beans and squash. Glenwood towns appear to have been rather stable. Each group remained in a given location for a period of time, moving only when nearby timber or tillable land became scarce. Archeologists believe that small bands of men hunted game in the immediate vicinity of their village to supplement the economy. Deer, elk, bison and other animals were taken. The local hunting practices of the Glenwood people seem to have differed markedly from the longer ranging communal hunts practiced by their neighbors called the Upper Republican who lived to the west.

Unlike the Mill Creek and Great Oasis peoples in western Iowa, the Glenwood people conducted very little trade. They did borrow some pottery making ideas from the Upper Republican and many Mississippian traits such as loop handles, lugs and effigy forms, but very few items of definite foreign origin have been recovered. Along with this lack of contact with the outside we find an apparent lack of enemies and warfare. No evidence has been found to indicate that any of the villages was fortified with stockade fences or dry moats. Such structures are found on some Mill Creek sites and even more commonly along the Missouri River in present-day South Dakota. Along with this lack of warfare we might expect the absence of military societies similar to those found among Plains Indians of the Historic Period.

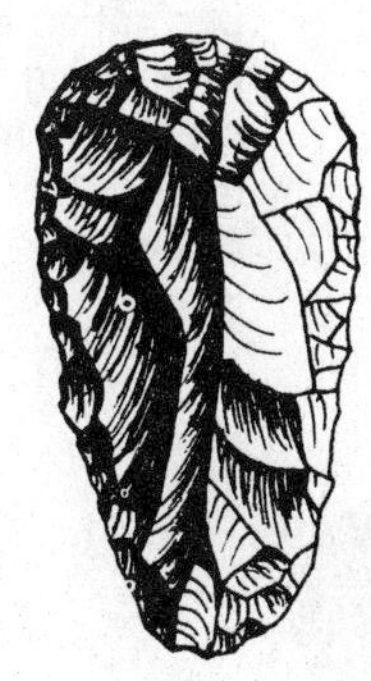

Hide scrapers of the Glenwood people are often long and oval in shape. Hide dressing tools of one kind or another are found among all peoples of Iowa from the earliest times. Some were hand held, while others were tied to large ribs, or antler tips. Microscopic studies of scratches on the blade indicate the manner in which specific specimens were used.

One variety of Glenwood pottery is shown at left. Several kinds of pots were produced. Ordinarily only fragments called "sherds" are found since vessels were kept in use until they were broken. (Shown one-half size.)

A plain Glenwood vessel with a slightly outcurving rim appears at right. Decoration around the rim was applied by pressing a stick or bone tool into the moist clay before firing in an open kiln made of sticks and perhaps dung. (Shown one-half size.)

Clay pipes are distinctive features of the Glenwood peoples not shared by other western Iowa cultures. This specimen features a snake effigy wrapped around the bowl. It is likely that the pipes performed some ritual function which indicates that tobacco may have been cultivated. (Shown slightly reduced.)

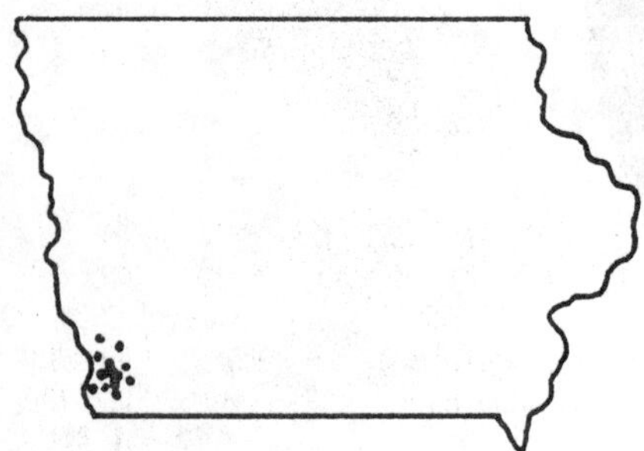

GLENWOOD SITES
IN SOUTHWESTERN IOWA

What can be said of the social life of these peoples? Our answers must be speculative in nature and based largely on analogy with historic peoples (e.g., Pawnee and Arikara), but some suggestions can be made. Each household was probably occupied by a territorially based lineage. A lineage is a group of related people including parents, grandparents, children and perhaps others who trace their inheritance to a known ancestor who lived only five or six generations earlier.

The members of a number of households in an area may have been linked together into a clan. Like the lineage, the clan is a social unit, only larger. The main difference

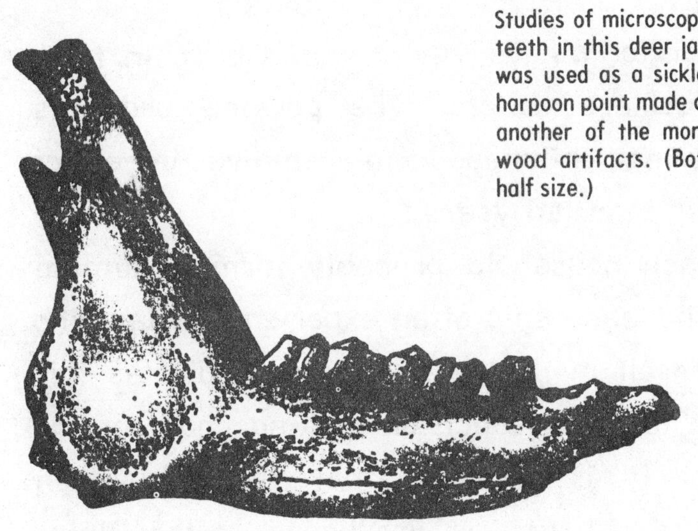

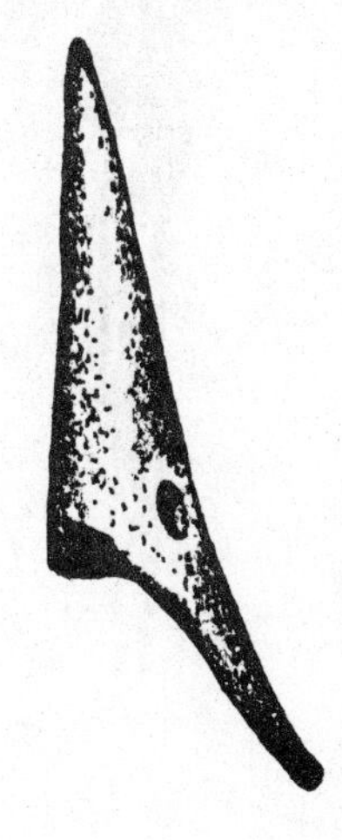

Studies of microscopic scratches on the teeth in this deer jaw indicate the tool was used as a sickle. The toggle head harpoon point made of antler represents another of the more distinctive Glenwood artifacts. (Both are shown one-half size.)

between the two lies in the fact that clan members are "related" to a common mythical ancestor—sometimes a bird, wolf or other animal. It is likely that two or more clans occupying an area were divided in such a way that one group would supply marriage partners for the other. Rules forbidding marriage to a member of one's own family are almost universal in the primitive as well as the civilized world.

We might speculate that if a young Glenwood pair were married the couple would either establish their home in the area of the bride's mother's house or move in with her. This would insure firm and lasting ties with the bride's lineage. In time it is likely that the bride's younger sisters might also marry her husband forming a polygynous family. This may seem unusual, but among many groups of primitive people women do not object to this arrangement. Additional wives become co-workers and

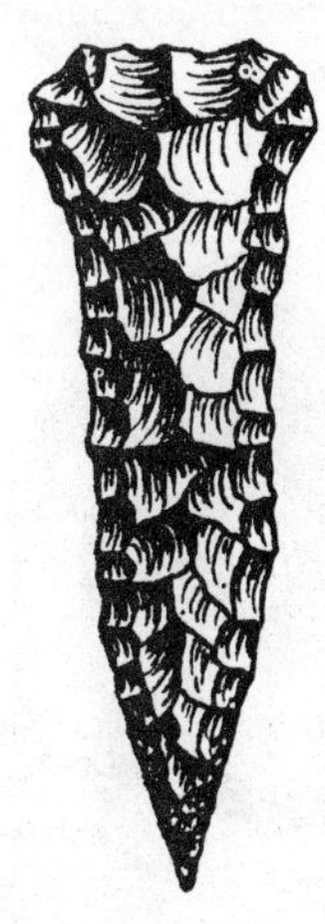

Artifacts called "drills" are found on many western Iowa sites. They have tapered blades with a diamond shaped to circular cross-section. They probably functioned as punching and drilling tools.

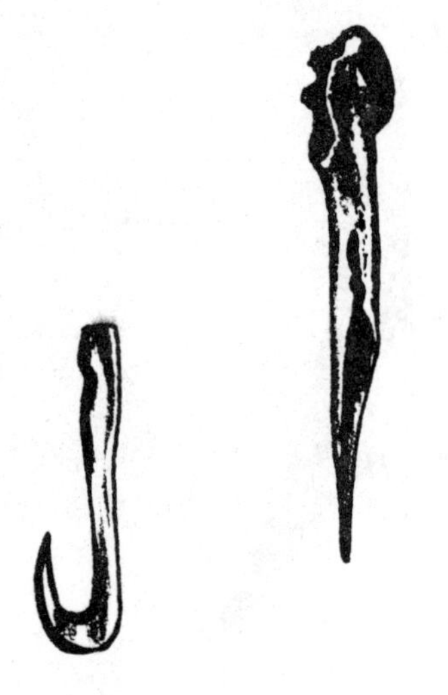

Items made of bone include fishhooks made from the toe bone of a deer, and an awl produced from a thin-walled wing bone of a medium sized bird.

Shell "hoes" were presumably used as digging and gardening tools. A short wooden handle may have been tied horizontally across the top, using the hole in the center. Although common in the Southeast, this tool type was not widely distributed in western Iowa beyond the Glenwood area. (Shown one-fourth size.)

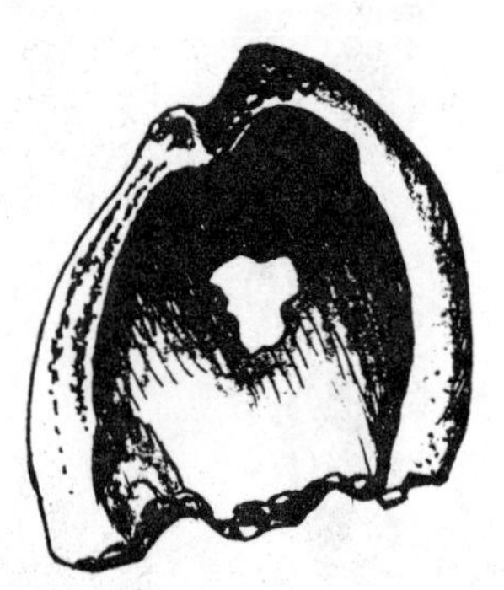

make life easier for all. Polygyny works best, in fact, when the wives are sisters. The pecking order is established during childhood and remains in effect throughout their married years.

Men from each household probably formed hunting parties under the leadership of an experienced man who had proven himself in the past. Headmen such as this would combine to be the decision making body for the entire village. It is unlikely that there was an authoritarian "chief" such as was known to the Plains nomads of the Historic Period. The lack of a large or specialized lodge within the village attests to a simple classless society dependent on a yearly hunting-gathering-farming cycle. Villages are not laid out with an orderly plan. There is no evidence of wealth based on trade and there was apparently no preferential treatment for the dead. Whatever status people had was earned during their lifetimes through skill, wisdom or some other desirable trait. For all cultures considered herein, it is best to think of persons of influence rather than persons of authority.

As time passed, the Glenwood peoples experienced increasing contact with Oneota peoples who were living in adjacent areas. To a lesser extent, changes were caused by their contacts with the Upper Republican neighbors farther to the west. Throughout the Glenwood occupation life seems to have changed little. Many of the tools they used were common to virtually all other plains and prairie groups—farming implements, hunting, fishing, hide-working tools and a variety of ornaments. A few items in use were more limited in distribution in Iowa including toggle head harpoon points, shell hoes and clay elbow pipes—occasionally with effigy figures on them.

The Glenwood culture disappeared from the ar-cheological record before the year A.D. 1400. Changing climatic, environmental and cultural factors probably put new pressures on the previously stable Glenwood hamlets. Ultimately the people were forced to move away. As they did they no doubt came into contact with new peoples and conditions that changed their lives and culture forever. It seems likely that the people themselves did not die out. They blended in with other groups and lost their cultural identity.

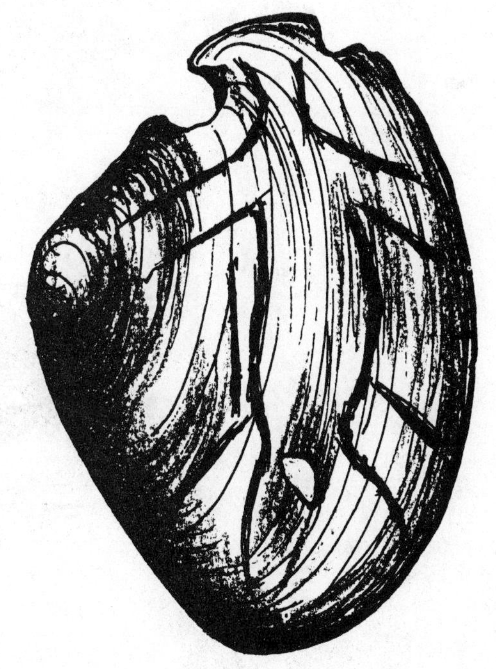

The freshwater clam shell below bears the incised design of a "thunderbird." It was recovered from the salvage excavation of a Glenwood house in Mills County. (Shown one-half size.)

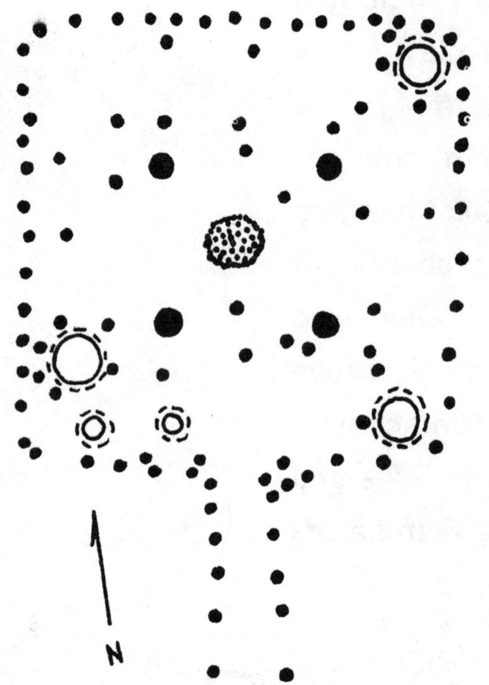

The floor plan of a Glenwood house appears at left. Structures were generally 30 feet square with four main roof supports and a south-facing entrance. Note undercut storage pits (dashed lines) and central fire pit. The houses may have had sod roofs as shown in the reconstruction below.

Sources and Suggested Readings

ANDERSON, ADRIAN D. (1954), Stone Artifacts from the Glenwood Area. Journal of the Iowa Archeological Society, Vol. 4, No. 2, pp. 2-16.

ANDERSON, ADRIAN D. (1961), The Glenwood Sequence. Journal of the Iowa Archeological Society, Vol. 10, No. 3, pp. 1-101.

BROWN, LIONEL A. (1967), Pony Creek Archaeology. Publications in Salvage Archeology, No. 5, River Basin Surveys, Smithsonian Institution.

DAVIS, DONALD D. (1959), Site O-32-5. Iowa Archeological Society Newsletter, No. 29, pp. 4-6.

DEAN, SETH (1883), Antiquities of Mills County, Iowa. Annual Report of the Smithsonian Institution, 1881, pp. 528-532.

GRADWOHL, DAVID M. (1969), Prehistoric Villages in Eastern Nebraska. Nebraska State Historical Society, Publications in Anthropology, No. 4.

IVES, JOHN C. (1955), Glenwood Ceramics. Journal of the Iowa Archeological Society, Vol. 4, Nos. 3-4, pp. 2-32.

PROUDFIT, S.V. (1881), Antiquities on the Missouri Bluffs. American Antiquarian, Vol. 3, pp. 271-280.

WOOD, W. RAYMOND, ed. (1969), Two House Sites in the Central Plains: An Experiment in Archaeology. Plains Anthropologist, Memoir No. 6.

ZIMMERMAN, LARRY J. (1971), The Glenwood Taxonomic Problem. Master's Thesis, University of Iowa, Iowa City.

Troubled Mill Creek

6

Of all the Late Prehistoric cultures considered here, Mill Creek was probably the most elaborate. Who were they? Where did they come from? How did they differ from other groups in the area? What can be said of their economy, settlement pattern and social organization?

The Mill Creek groups seem to be Mississippian, resembling this culture even more strongly than the Glenwood groups discussed previously. Judging from their limited distribution and the wide variety of pottery styles and other artifact categories it appears to some researchers that the Mill Creek groups colonized the Big Sioux and Little Sioux River valleys from the great Mississippian centers of Aztalan in southern Wisconsin or Cahokia in southern Illinois. Others believe the Mill Creek

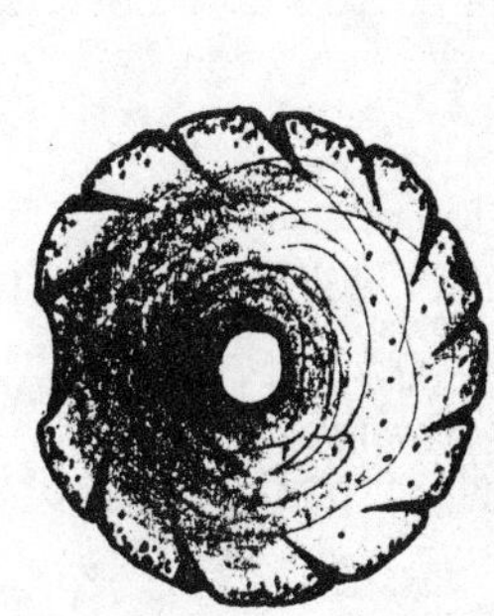

The ear spool above, made from the backbone of a large fish, was probably worn by an important Mill Creek person. The artifact is unique to the area and may have been traded from the southern Plains. (Front and side views shown.)

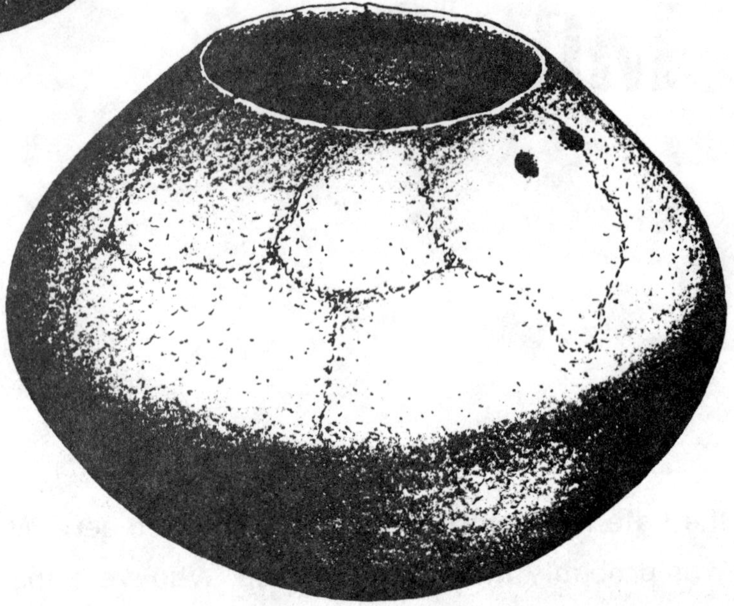

Mill Creek bowls often have effigy heads and tails. They may have served some ritual purpose in clan rights. The "seed jar" at right has holes for suspension. Most are colored red with an iron rich clay "slip" applied to the outside of the pots before firing. (Both vessels shown one-half size.)

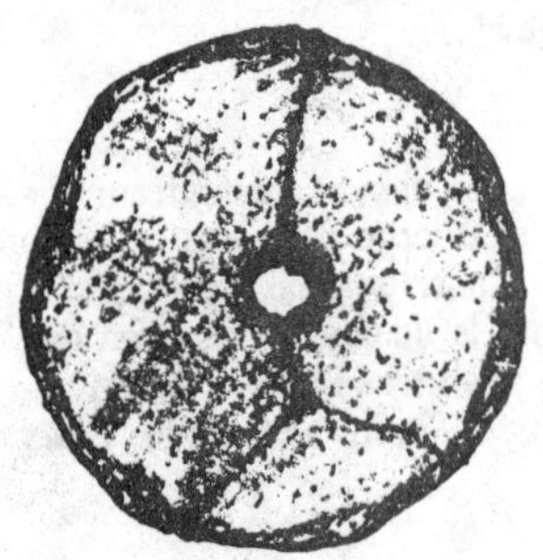

Circular objects made of clay are common on Mill Creek sites. The one above is made of a piece of broken pottery. The three beads are fired lumps of clay — perhaps part of a necklace. Perforated discs like the one shown below are commonly called "spindle whorls."

culture to be of local origin under strong Mississippian influence. Whatever the case, they appeared in northwest Iowa about A.D. 900 and began to blend with local cultures—primarily the developing Great Oasis, but to a lesser extent other late Woodland peoples.

Mill Creek differs from the Great Oasis population in that they possessed a much wider variety of artifacts. They made bowls; collared, rimless and high-rimmed jars; and effigy forms and "S"-rimmed jars. The Great Oasis peoples produced only one flared-rim and one collared-rim variety. Mill Creek potters abandoned the

Woodland and Great Oasis tradition of cord roughening the bodies of their pots and began the practice of smoothing and sometimes "trailing" the exteriors of vessels.

The settlement pattern of Mill Creek peoples often involved long-term occupation and sometimes reoccupation of sites. New houses were built over old, causing the accumulation of deep mounds reminiscent of the "tells" of the Near East on a small scale. The deposits of Great Oasis and Glenwood villages by contrast are thin and scattered and the sites generally are found in locations

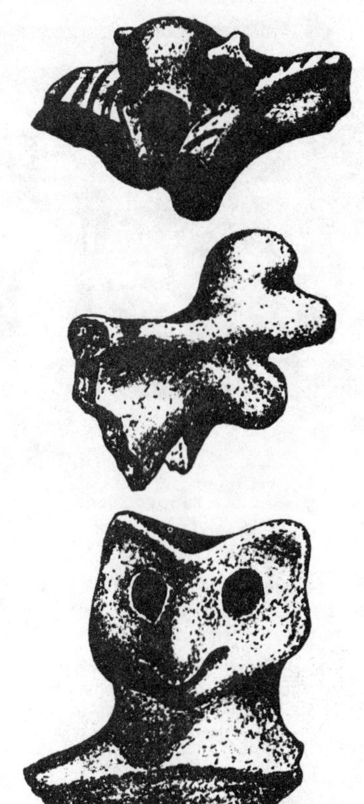

Effigies are found on jars as well as bowls. From top to bottom, these appear to resemble a raccoon (some have striped tails!), a human form and a bird of prey.

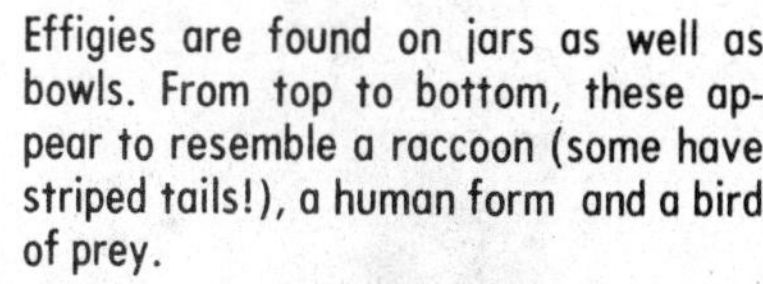

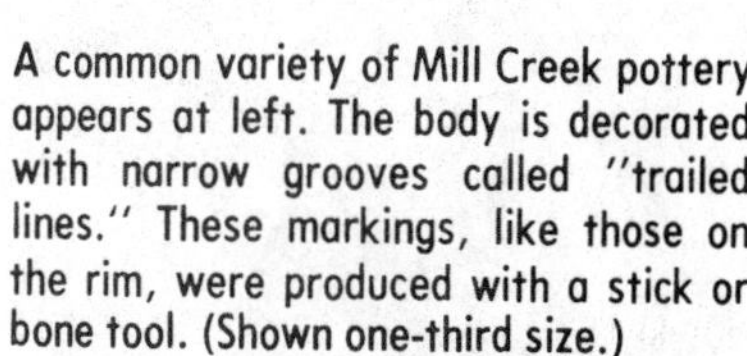

A common variety of Mill Creek pottery appears at left. The body is decorated with narrow grooves called "trailed lines." These markings, like those on the rim, were produced with a stick or bone tool. (Shown one-third size.)

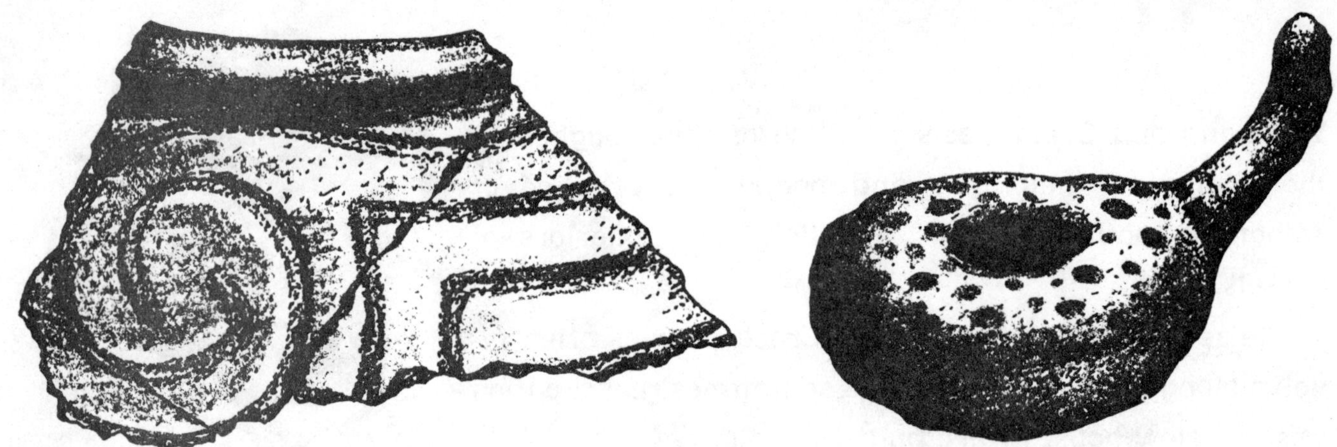

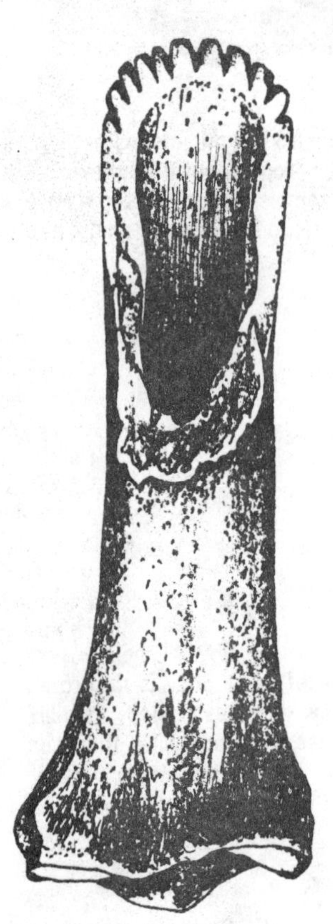

The highly polished black rim fragment above represents a definite trade vessel from the great Mississippian center called "Cahokia," located near present-day East St. Louis, Illinois. The "miniature pot" at right is unique. It features black paint spots around the opening; its purpose is unknown. Some miniature pots of the Mill Creek may be children's toys or "practice pots."

The toothed "flesher" (left) is made from the lower leg bone of a bison. It is a common type of scraping tool along the Missouri River in the Dakotas. (Shown one-half size.)

that could not be defended. Many Mill Creek villages appear to have been fortified—a unique feature in western Iowa. If they had enemies, who were they? Our best guess is their Oneota neighbors to the south (see Chapter 7).

It seems likely that the tightly knit Mill Creek villages with their scattered garden plots and caches of corn occasionally fell victim to raiding bands of Oneota. The Oneota are singled out as the villains because they were contemporaries of the Mill Creek and yet there is virtually no mixture of artifacts, indicating that trade did not take place between the two groups. This is not the case with the Great Oasis where we find good evidence of face-to-face contact and exchange of goods and ideas.

The economy of the Mill Creek was based on the cultivation of corn, beans and squash. Animal bones and other remains found on the sites indicate that hunting, trapping, fishing and gathering were of nearly equal importance. As one might expect, the plants and animals used reflect the local ecology and underscore the peoples'

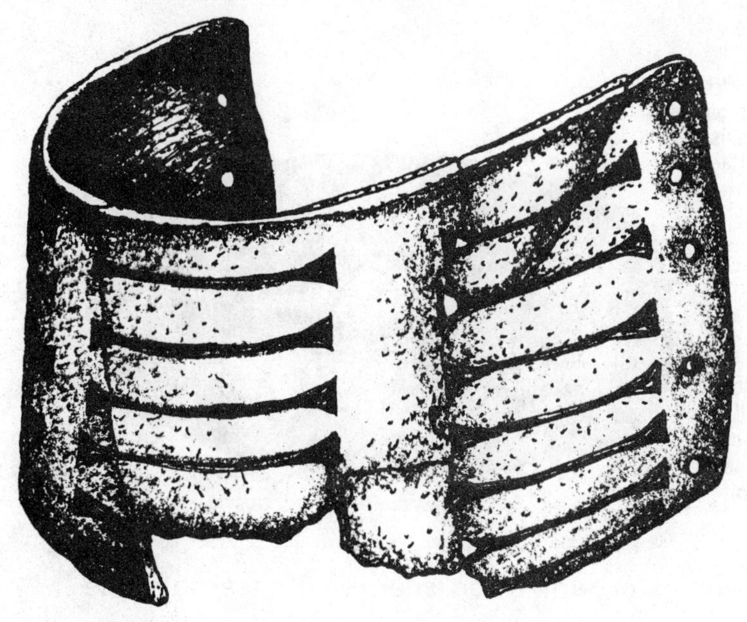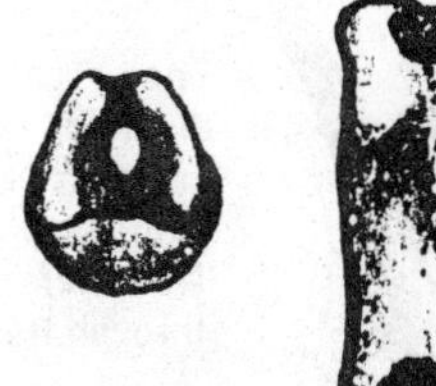

Mill Creek bone objects are often rather elaborate. The "arm guard" at left was made from a section of bison hip bone. It was warped into shape by soaking. The deer toe bone above was cut and drilled (front and end views). It may have been a "bangle" or bead, but similar bones were used in the "cup and pin" game played by Historic Plains groups.

The bone awl at left may have been a leather punch or basketry making tool. The blunt splinter at right was a flint knapper used to make arrow points and other stone tools.

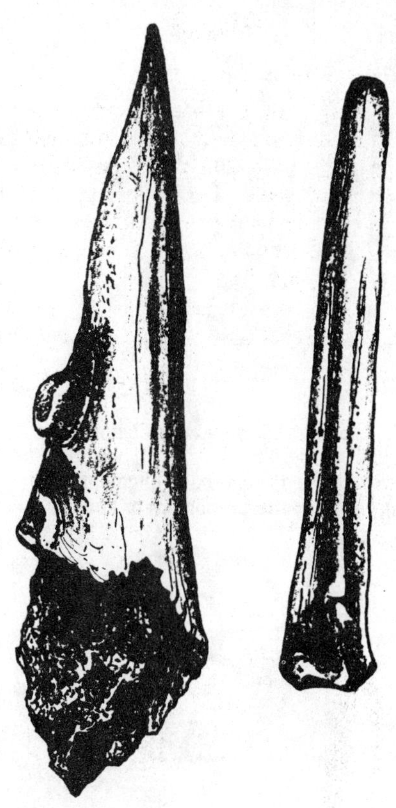

close reliance on the environment. Bird bones found at a site on the Little Sioux, for example, consisted primarily of woodland species and birds of prey with some prairie and marsh types. Aquatic bird bones were in the minority. A Great Oasis site near the Big Sioux River showed a reverse trend with the greatest emphasis on aquatic species—primarily migratory types of the Missouri Flyway.

Rodent bones, particularly pocket gopher, are abundant in many sites. Although they were generally considered to be late intrusions, an analysis at one site has shown that many were food items. Skulls and long bones are often cut and burned—presumably these rodents were butchered and eaten. Other studies similar to those discussed above in connection with Great Oasis cache pits have been conducted on Mill Creek sites resulting in the discovery of still other food remains. Middens are more difficult to excavate and interpret than single houses due to mixing of materials over long occupational periods.

The "chunkey" or "door knob discoidal" was probably used in a game played by Late Woodland and Mississippian peoples in Missouri and Illinois. This item may have been obtained through trade.

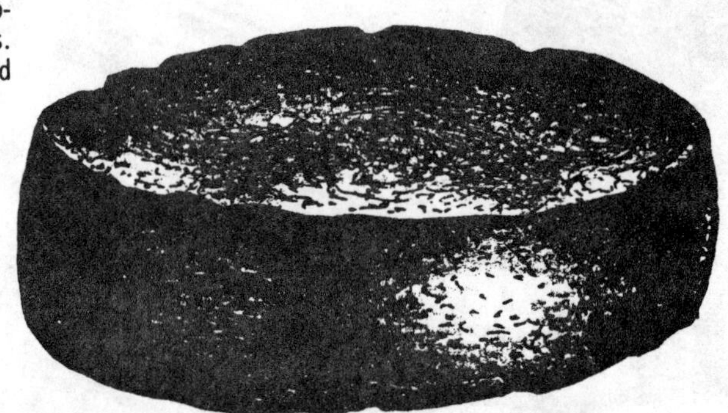

Bone "pins" and "matting needles" are occasionally found — although usually in pieces. Their exact functions are not known. These complete specimens came from Cherokee County. (Shown one-half size.)

The perforated bone disc below was found in Cherokee County. It was painted with red, iron-oxide pigment and may have been an ornament or button.

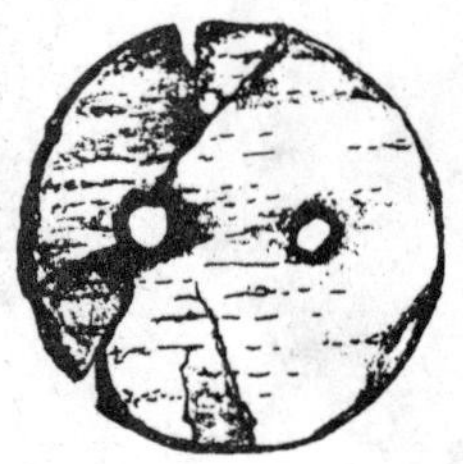

Mill Creek social organization seems to resemble the Glenwood and Great Oasis patterns although it may have been more elaborate. Some Mill Creek villages show evidence of a considerable amount of planning. One of the Plymouth County sites excavated by pioneer archeologist Ellison Orr appears to have had houses lined up in a row. Still others are fortified. The Wittrock Site in O'Brien County even features ramps and bastions more reminiscent of Initial Middle Missouri sites along the Missouri River in South Dakota. Taken together these features indicate a greater degree of social control. Mill Creek houses are poorly known, although it can be said that they were large rectangular structures similar to those described for the Great Oasis culture with subfloor storage pits, mud-plastered walls and grass roofs. Each house probably contained an extended family consisting of several men, women and children. Such a unit would have the advantage of spreading out the economic risks by providing more manpower thus making a wider range of activities possible.

Like Glenwood and Great Oasis, tight clusters of pottery making techniques are best conceived in a system of inheritance centered around the women's line of descent. Nevertheless, a certain amount of variation in pottery can be expected. It is in part due to experimentation and attempts to copy trade wares. It is also possible that some wives were captured or purchased from beyond the local group. These women would integrate their own pottery making methods into the tradition of the Mill Creek culture and provide a mechanism for gradual change. Ordinarily change comes slowly among primitive

MILL CREEK SITES
IN NORTHWESTERN IOWA

Pipes are rare among the Mill Creek. The tubular form and elbow pipe below are both made of red pipestone. Since this material was sacred to later tribes, it is likely that Mill Creek pipes were used for ceremonial purposes.

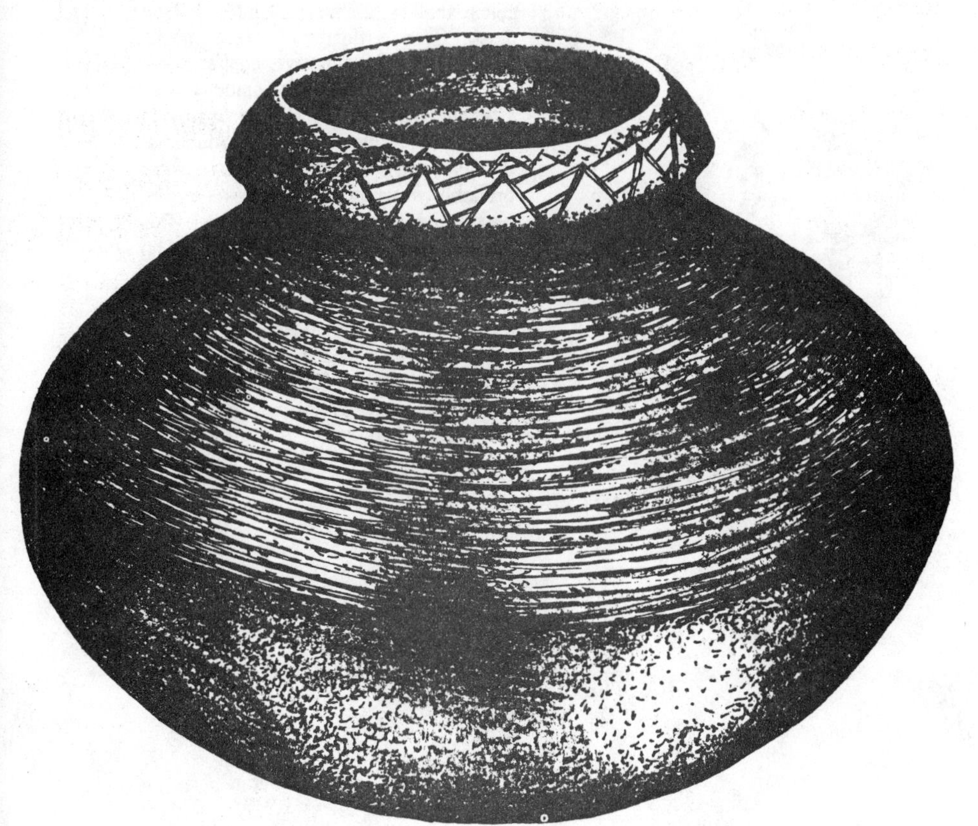

The "S"-rim pottery form is so-named because the rim doubles back on itself at the mouth of the vessel. Although invariably present on Mill Creek sites, this form is always a very minor type. The "S"-rim seems to occur more commonly in South Dakota. (Shown one-half size.)

peoples, for they are not inclined to criticize or challenge their cultures—their styles are ritualized and accepted by all. Therefore, once the Mill Creek pattern of life became established and adjusted to the local environment it became rather stable and changed little over a period of several hundred years. Ultimately, due to changing climatic conditions and perhaps pressure from their Oneota neighbors, they were forced to leave northwest Iowa. No one knows where they went.

Mill Creek arrow points are quite variable. Their small size and frequent "poor workmanship" reflects the low quality of available stone. Most rocks used to make stone tools were obtained from glacial gravels along the streambeds of the Big Sioux and Little Sioux Rivers and their tributaries.

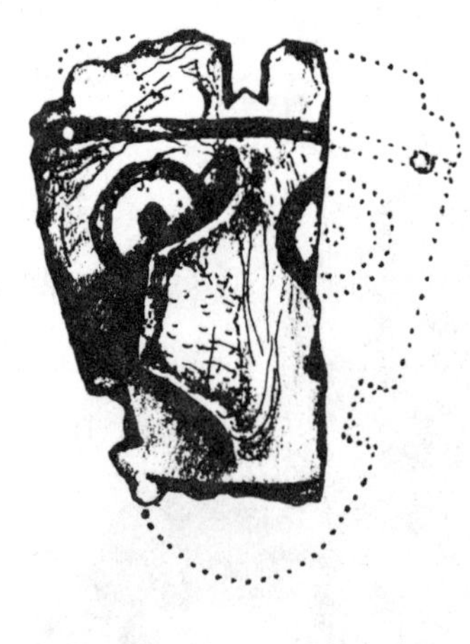

This object, made of a large marine conch shell, is called a Long-Nosed God mask. Over a dozen of these masks made of shell or native copper have been found in Mississippian-related sites in the eastern United States in Louisiana, Florida, Tennessee, Alabama, Illinois and Wisconsin. They were probably worn as ear ornaments by important religious practitioners. This mask, found on the surface of a Mill Creek site in Cherokee County by an amateur archeologist, is the only one known from Iowa. It is important in demonstrating that Mississippian exchanges with the Mill Creek people involved ideology as well as technology and material goods.

Sources and Suggested Readings

ANDERSON, DUANE C. (1969). Mill Creek Culture: A Review. Plains Anthropologist, Vol. 14, No. 44, pp. 137-143.

ANDERSON, DUANE C. (1972), The Ceramic Complex at the Brewster Site (13CK15): A Mill Creek Component in Northwestern Iowa. Ph.D. Dissertation, University of Colorado, Boulder.

ANDERSON, DUANE C. (1973), Brewster Site (13CK15): Lithic Analysis. Journal of the Iowa Archeological Society, Vol. 20, pp. 1-75.

FLANDERS, RICHARD E. (1960), A Re-examination of Mill Creek Ceramics: The Robinson Technique. Journal of the Iowa Archeological Society, Vol. 10, No. 2, pp. 1-34.

FUGLE, EUGENE M. 1962), Mill Creek Culture and Technology. Journal of the Iowa Archeological Society, Vol. 11, No. 4, pp. 1-126.

HENNING, DALE R., ed. (1968-69), Climatic Change and the Mill Creek Culture of Iowa: Parts 1 and 2. Journal of the Iowa Archeological Society, Vol. 18, pp. 6-12.

HENNING, DALE R. (1971), Origins of Mill Creek. Journal of the Iowa Archeological Society, Vol. 18, pp. 6-12.

IVES, JOHN C. (1955), Mill Creek Pottery. Journal of the Iowa Archeological Society, Vol. 11, No. 3, pp. 1-59.

SEMKEN, HOLMES A. (1971), Small Mammal Remains from the Wittrock Mill Creek Culture Site. In Prehistoric Investigations, Marshall McKusick (ed.), Office of the State Archaelogist, Report No. 3, pp. 109-113.

VIS, ROBERT B. and DALE R. HENNING (1969), A Local Sequence for Mill Creek Sites in the Little Sioux River Valley. Plains Anthropologist, Vol. 14, No. 46, pp. 253-271.

ZIMMERMAN, LARRY J. (1971), Skadeland Mill Creek Culture Site. In Prehistoric Investigations, Marshall McKusick (ed.), Office of the State Archaeologist, Report No. 3, pp. 114-124.

Ancestors of the Ioway

7

Some time before A.D. 950 a broad cultural tradition called Oneota was spreading across much of Minnesota, Wisconsin, Illinois, Missouri, eastern Nebraska and Iowa. The people adapted to a variety of habitats and occupied the Midwest until the onset of the Historic Period over 600 years later. When European traders and trappers began moving in during the French Colonial Period, these groups emerged as various Siouan speaking tribes including the Winnebago, Missouri, Osage, Little Osage, Kansa, Oto and Ioway. In the state of Iowa prehistoric Oneota populations are believed to have given rise to the Ioway and perhaps the Oto tribes. The earliest chapter of Oneota prehistory began in western Iowa in the vicinity of Correctionville in Woodbury County.

Here, in an area on the periphery of the Mill Creek and Great Oasis dominated territory, the Oneota lived

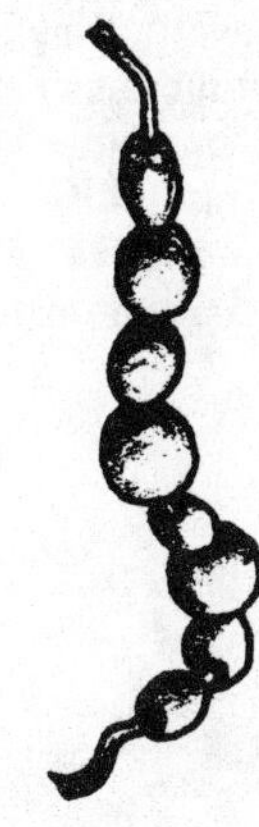

Blue glass trade beads are definite indications of European contact. Trade items such as these help to distinguish Historic Ioway sites from prehistoric Oneota villages.

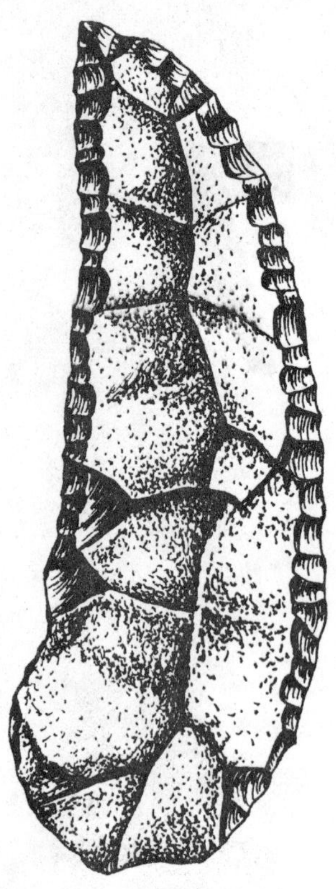

This cutting tool was made of an olive-green stone called "Bijou Hills Quartzite" from South Dakota. This material was used somewhat more commonly by Oneota peoples than other western Iowa cultures. This difference in preference may be indicative of trade in which Mill Creek and Great Oasis did not participate.

periodically for some 400 years. During this time they apparently did not trade with Mill Creek or Great Oasis peoples nor were they influenced by their cultures. Studies indicate that sites were occupied, abandoned and reoccupied again and again testifying to a more nomadic way of life than their northern neighbors. Villages were not fortified and no house structures are known, although they most certainly existed. They raised corn and perhaps other crops and, judging from the number of pipes found on sites, tobacco was also cultivated.

It may have been the Oneota pattern of periodic movement with emphasis on hunting and raiding that enabled them to survive in the area while the more settled cultures could not. The story is incomplete, due in part to the history of the Correctionville studies. The main sites were destroyed almost entirely by gravel operations in the late 1950's. The archeological work was done by volunteers under difficult salvage conditions in a very

Bumps and irregularities were trimmed from arrow shafts with a pair of sandstone abraders like the one shown below. Complete specimens are rare, but fragments are common and can be recognized by the "U"-shaped groove in the center.

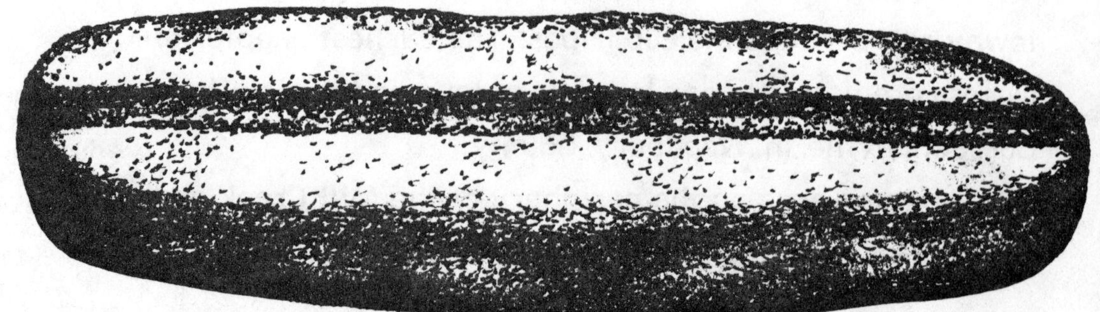

Oneota peoples used pipestone pipes and ''tablets'' for religious purposes. The one at left features the ''weeping eye'' design widely recognized in the southeastern United States. Feathers or other perishable material may have been attached to the top of the head where a rough platform appears. The disc bowl pipe below was another popular Oneota form.

limited period of time. Unfortunately, rumors of continuing vandalism in the area persist to this day.

One of the most interesting aspects of these peoples is the fact that their pottery vessels defy classification into neat categories. In the case of the Mill Creek and Great Oasis cultures it is possible to name ''types'' based on clusters of decorative traits applied to vessels. Why is this not possible for the Oneota? Let us recall that in the case of Mill Creek, Great Oasis and Glenwood the social organization was such that when a couple was married they went to live with the bride's mother's family. Women who were related lived together, worked together and learned together and therefore perpetuated much uniformity in the ceramic tradition. No new females

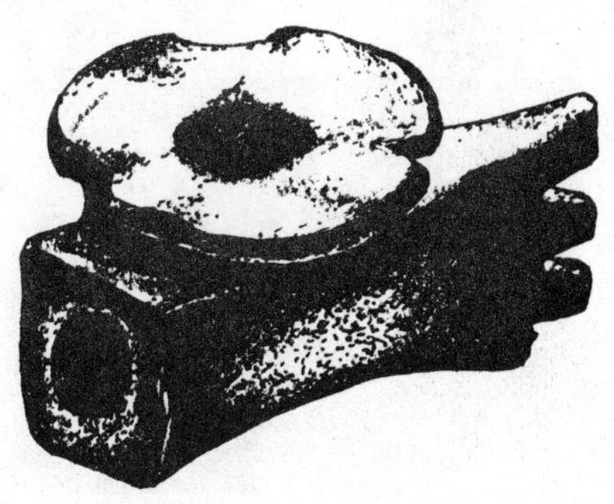

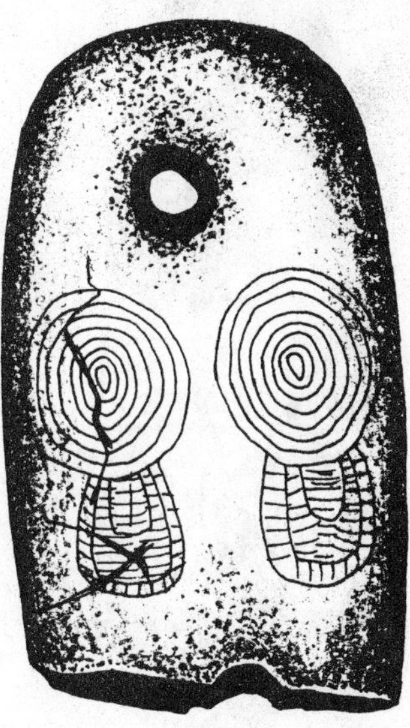

The pipestone gorget below may be an Oneota artifact. It was found in the bed of Elm Creek in Harrison County. The item features two drilled holes and may have been worn as an ornament. The meaning of the circular motifs is not known.

Well-shaped, full-grooved mauls were used by the Oneota as sledge hammers for driving stakes and other tasks around the village. The groove was used to tie on a wooden handle secured with rawhide. Although these ''mauls'' were used by other cultures, most were not as well made or as symmetrical as those of the Oneota. (Shown one-half size.)

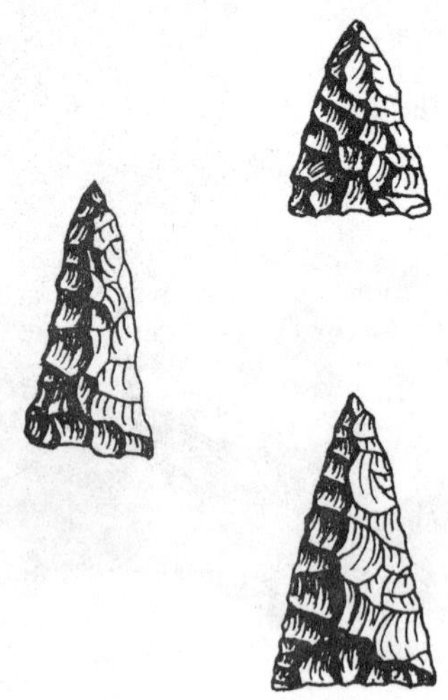

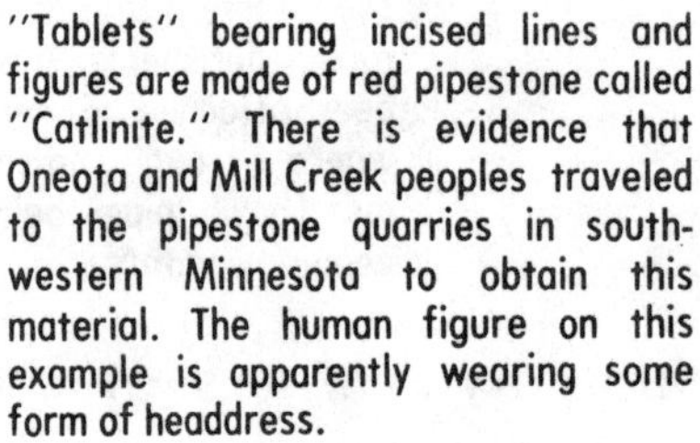

''Tablets'' bearing incised lines and figures are made of red pipestone called ''Catlinite.'' There is evidence that Oneota and Mill Creek peoples traveled to the pipestone quarries in south-western Minnesota to obtain this material. The human figure on this example is apparently wearing some form of headdress.

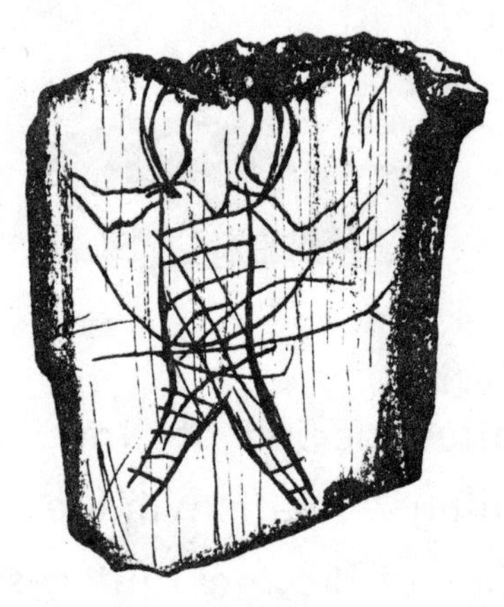

Arrow points of the Oneota are often triangular and unnotched. The ''knife'' below is a common variety of tool on Oneota sites.

would enter a household with new ideas except in relatively rare cases of brides who were captured or purchased from beyond the local area.

It appears that the Oneota reckoned their descent through the father's side of the family. In this system, young married people resided in the groom's father's household or perhaps in a new residence established nearby. If this interpretation is correct, it means that the males living together were related and the females were not. The pottery they made was a blend of designs and techniques learned both before and after marriage. In short, there was no single way of doing things. A variety of possibilities presented themselves. Some overall ideas were held in common such as the use of crushed clam shell in the paste for temper, general shape of the vessel and curvature of the rim. But there was no preconceived method of applying designs, no specified number of handles, arrangement of dots or lines. These elements were applied at random. No mother or sister was standing by to point out the ''proper'' way to decorate a pot to make it look like all other pots. This so-called "patrilocal residence pattern," thought to be responsible for this ceramic diversity, was found to be in use by the Ioway Indians in historic times.

By A.D. 1400 the Mill Creek and Great Oasis had abandoned northwestern Iowa. Soon after, the Oneota occupied a site north of Cherokee in the heart of former Mill Creek territory. It seems to link earlier Oneota peoples with eastern Iowa groups which persisted into the historic era. The Oneota culture derives its name from sites described as early as 1914 on the Upper Iowa River in northeastern Iowa. The river was formerly known as the Oneota River. Some of the eastern sites have produced trade items of glass and metal indicating that they were in contact at least indirectly with Europeans. The Oneota at

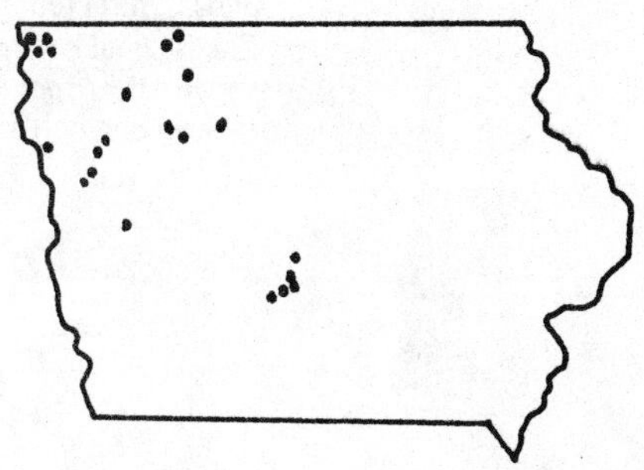

ONEOTA SITES
IN WESTERN IOWA

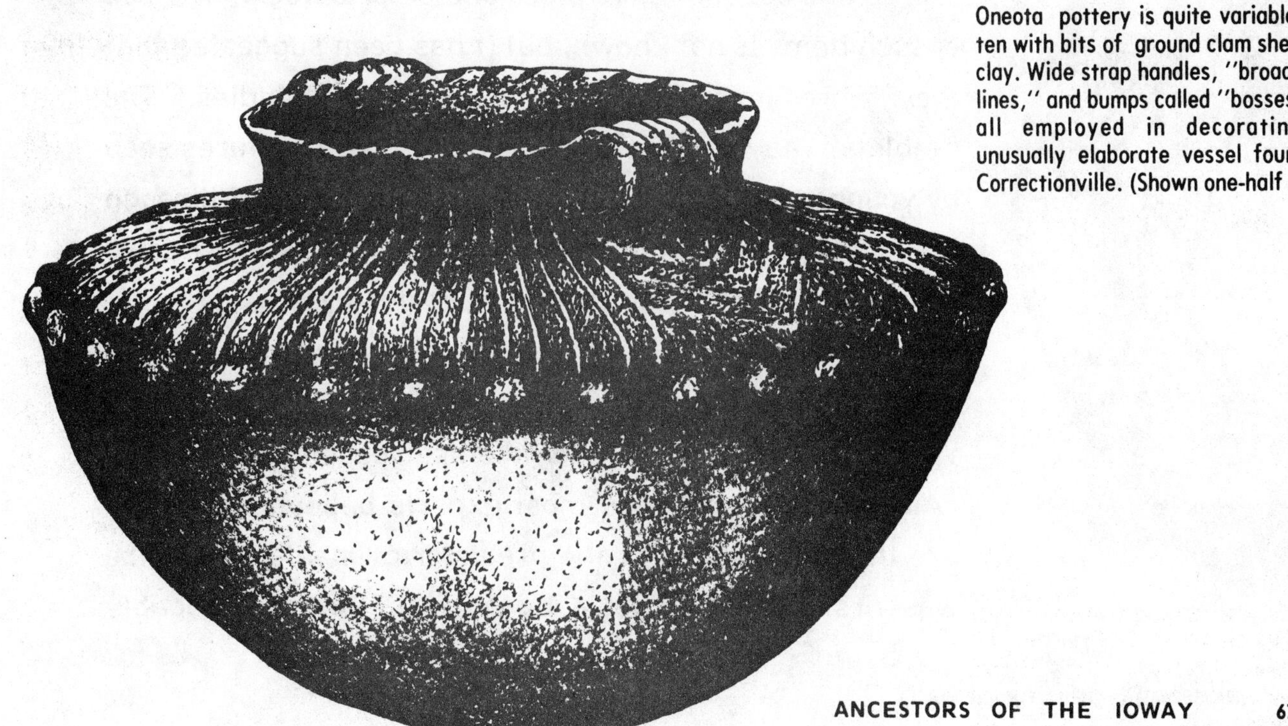

Oneota pottery is quite variable — often with bits of ground clam shell in the clay. Wide strap handles, "broad trailed lines," and bumps called "bosses" were all employed in decorating this unusually elaborate vessel found near Correctionville. (Shown one-half size.)

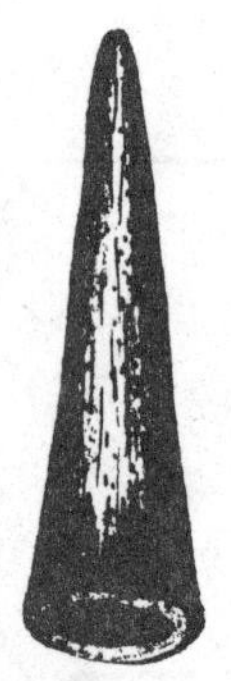

Hollowed antler arrow points (left) are occasionally found on Oneota sites. The worn base of a deer antler (right) was used as a flint knapper's hammer. Blows directed along the edge of flakes would remove chips and help to shape the tool being manufactured. (Shown one-half size.)

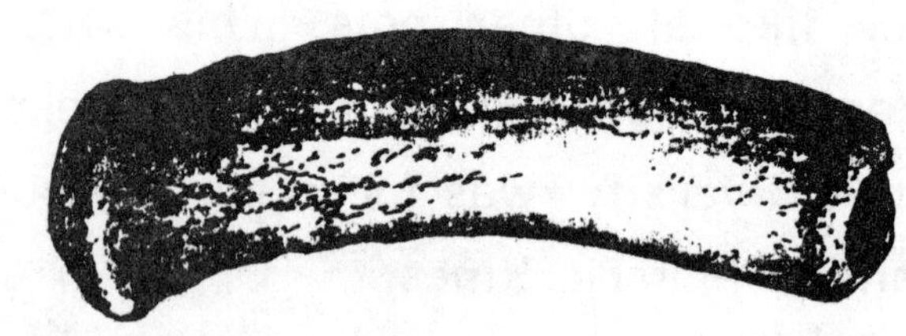

The item below was probably a tool used to scrape the inside of a pottery vessel during manufacture. It was made of a bison shoulder blade and has a human form scratched lightly into the surface.

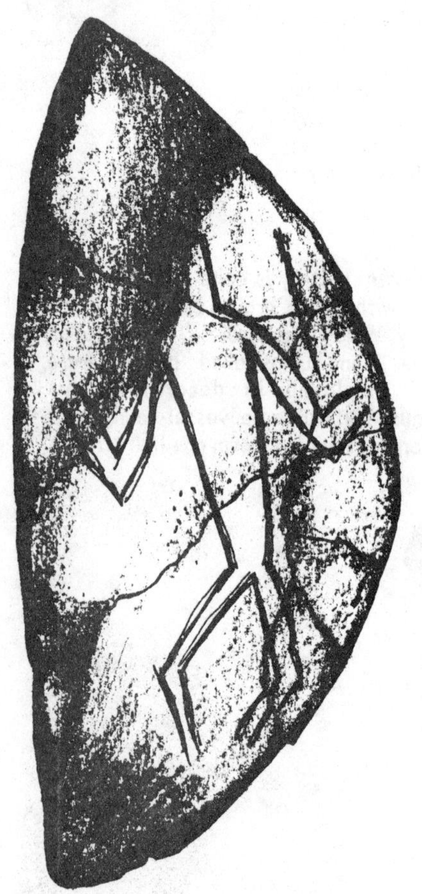

this time were also known from several western Iowa counties including Clay, Lyon and Buena Vista. As history began to overtake the Oneota they started to change as a result of pressures from Europeans and developing Plains Indians groups. A period of spotty documentation and social change and much movement followed the Oneota into the history books.

One of the hallmarks of Oneota culture lies in their use of red pipestone called Catlinite obtained from the quarries in southwestern Minnesota. The material was sacred and used to make pipes and other objects. The use of such items is not known, but it has been suggested that they were incorporated into medicine bundles. The "tablets" may carry records of mythical creatures seen by young men on the vision quest as they passed through their puberty initiation rites. Similar tablets are known from northeastern Missouri and eastern Iowa.

In 1676 Father Louis Andre described a few members of a "large but poor tribe" who visited him at Green Bay, Wisconsin, and identified themselves as the Ioway (Aiaoua) Indians. Now, most experts believe the Ioway are the descendants of the prehistoric Oneota. The tribe was first visited in Iowa by Nicolas Perrot (probably along the Upper Iowa River) in 1685. At that time they were still cooking in earthen pots. Then, as time passed, the tribe was variously reported at several locations including the Iowa Lakes Region, the Big Sioux River, the area near Council Bluffs, the Mississippi River in southeast Iowa, the Des Moines River, the Grand River in southwestern Iowa and finally near Keokuk.

The Ioway signed a treaty in 1830 with the United States government in which they gave up their Iowa land. They were then moved to the area of present northwestern Missouri where they remained until 1836. Reservation life began in 1837 when they were moved to a tract on the Nebraska-Kansas line adjacent to the Missouri River. The group began to fragment in the 1870's when the more traditional members of the tribe began drifting into Indian Territory—present-day Oklahoma. In 1883 this group

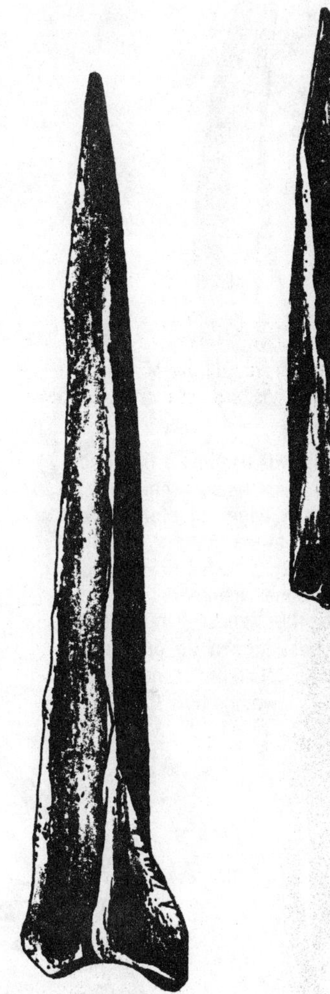

Bone awls of the Oneota were made from split longbones of large animals (left) as well as hollow bird bones.

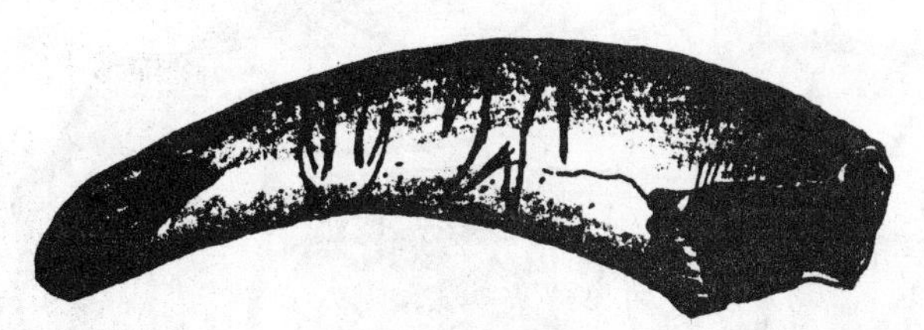

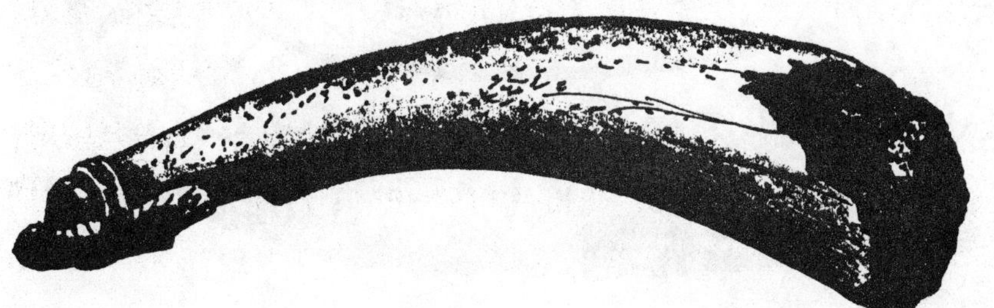

Antler tips were used as handles for hide-scraping tools. The one above features two incised human figures. The stone blade was tied to a flattened surface near the tip with rawhide as shown below. The blades received hard use and were often resharpened. (Shown one-half size.)

was given their own reservation, but it was taken back by the government just seven years later. Much of what is known of the Ioway's native culture as recorded during this time by missionaries and ethnographers. Now Ioway language and culture is extinct and its remaining people have been almost completely assimilated into American culture.

This antler tip was used as a flint knapper's tool. Chips were removed by pressing on the edges of stone flakes with the tip of the antler. The flint knapper's tool kit included flakers, hammerstones, bone hammers, abrasive stones and other items. A new branch of science has grown up around the study of the ancient stoneworker's technology. (Shown one-half size.)

This elaborate "catlinite tablet" bears the incised design of the mythical "water monster." It may have been carried in a medicine bundle by the ancestors of the Historic Ioway. (Shown two-thirds size.)

Sources and Suggested Readings

ANDERSON, DUANE C. (1973), Ioway Ethnohistory: A Review, Parts 1 and 2. Annals of Iowa, Vol. 41, No. 8, pp. 1228-1241 and Vol. 42, No. 1, pp. 41-59.

BRAY, ROBERT T. (1963), Southern Cult Motifs from the Utz Oneota Site, Saline County, Missouri. Missouri Archaeologist, Vol. 25, pp. 1-40.

HENNING, DALE R. (1961), Oneota Ceramics in Iowa. Journal of the Iowa Archaeological Society, Vol. 11, No. 2, pp. 1-60.

HENNING, DALE R. (1970), Development and Interrelationships of Oneota Culture in the Lower Missouri River Valley. Missouri Archaeologist, Vol. 32, pp. 1-180.

McKUSICK, MARSHALL, (1973), The Grant Oneota Village. Office of the State Archaeologist, Report No. 4.

MOTT, MILDRED (1938), The Relation of Historic Indian Tribes to Archaeological Manifestations in Iowa. Iowa Journal of History and Politics, Vol. 36, No. 3, pp. 227-304.

SKINNER, ALANSON (1915), Societies of the Iowa, Kansa and Ponca Indians. Anthropological Papers of the American Museum of Natural History, Vol. 11, Part 9, pp. 679-740.

SKINNER, ALANSON (1926), Ethnology of the Iowa Indians. Milwaukee Museum Bulletin, Vol. 5, No. 4, pp. 181-354.

STRAFFIN, DEAN (1971), The Kingston Oneota Site. Office of the State Archaeologist, Report No. 2.

WEDEL, MILDRED MOTT(1959), Oneota Sites on the Upper Iowa River. Missourri Archaeologist, Vol. 21, Nos. 2-4, pp. 1-181.

WEDEL, MILDRED MOTT (1961), Indian Villages on the Upper Iowa River. Palimpsest, Vol. 42, No. 12, pp. 561-592.

The Territory Beyond **8**

State lines impose artificial boundaries on research and tend to limit our understanding of cultural relationships. Since the responsibilities of state agencies usually stop at state lines and state laws vary considerably, researchers tend to be somewhat provincial. Further, communication is often best conducted on a state-wide level where professionals and amateurs are often better acquainted. All these factors point out how dangerous it is to think solely in terms of cultural developments in western Iowa. For a fuller understanding it is important that we at least explore the cultures in surrounding areas.

The earliest hunters were representatives of a widespread way of life common to much of the plains, prairies and woodlands, and cultural differences from place to place are not obvious. A considerable amount of uniformity existed among Woodland populations as well. It is noteworthy, however, that two Woodland variants, located along both sides of the Missouri River, differed from other so-called Hopewellian Woodland peoples discussed in Chapter 3. These are known as the Sterns Creek and Missouri Bluffs peoples. Both probably predate settled village life that began after A.D. 900.

While the Mill Creek culture is limited to four north-western Iowa counties, similar materials are found along the James and Missouri Rivers in southeastern South Dakota. The poorly known Over Focus is one of the Initial Middle Missouri groups believed to be contemporaneous with Mill Creek. These sites lack deep middens, but houses, pottery and other artifact types have many parallels.

We have said that Great Oasis culture extends north into Minnesota and west into South Dakota. In view of the concentration of materials in Plymouth County, it is in-conceivable that it does not occur in adjacent counties in Nebraska. Moving to the central part of Iowa, we find that Great Oasis pottery is not as elaborate and the collared-rim form not as abundant. In the future it may be necessary to break the culture down into subgroups to accommodate differences over wide areas.

The Glenwood culture is but a local variant of the Nebraska culture composed of early and late subdivisions extending from Doniphan, Kansas, up the Missouri River to Homer, Nebraska. The Glenwood culture of Iowa can only be understood in the broader context of the Nebraska phase.

The St. Helena culture occupied northeastern Nebraska at a time that probably postdates the disappearance of the Mill Creek and Great Oasis peoples from adjacent Iowa. These peoples were apparently in contact with Oneota and Initial Middle Missouri peoples of southwestern South Dakota, although their houses resemble more nearly those of the Nebraska culture. Their grit-tempered pottery featured a high percentage of collared rims. Loop handles appear on straight rims and the bodies of pots feature pronounced cord roughening and variable trailed designs.

In south central Minnesota the Cambria village and related camps were occupied from A.D. 1000-1300. Many traits are shared with western Iowa cultures, but there is little direct evidence of trade. Their economy appears to have been based largely on corn farming and they lived in the familiar long, rectangular earth-lodges. Their pottery has strong Mississippian appearance with some wares resembling flared-rim and collared-rim Mill Creek types.

The Steed Kisker culture of northwest Missouri is another Mississippian culture related in some way to the Nebraska culture. They had rounded houses with four main roof supports and a central fire pit reminiscent of the Glenwood as discussed in Chapter 5. They also used perforated shell hoes, triangular, side-notched arrow points and a variety of other stone and bone tools that would not be out of place on many western Iowa sites.

In eastern Iowa, mound builders of the Late Woodland Period tended to be replaced by the Oneota for the most part. Only one Oneota site has been excavated in southeastern Iowa, dating between A.D. 1200-1400. In time it is likely that still more Oneota sites will be investigated adding still more time depth to Oneota in the eastern part of Iowa.

All the cultures discussed in this book developed in a prehistoric culture area in which groups interacted and influenced one another with the passage of time. These cultures lived through changing climatic and environmental conditions as well as changing cultural conditions. Hunters occupied Iowa for the first few thousand years following the Ice Age. The hunting and foraging way of life persisted until with the Woodland peoples the knowledge of pottery making and farming began to spread into the area. By A.D. 900 climatic conditions had adjusted favorably to allow farming and the establishment of settled village life. During this time, resident Woodland peoples gave rise to the Great Oasis while other groups under strong influence from the Mississippian heartland became the Mill Creek and Glenwood cultures. A different wave of peoples and ideas from the Mississippian source area gave rise to the Oneota at this same time.

By A.D. 1250 the optimum climatic conditions so favorable to these villagers began to deteriorate with a decrease in warm moist summer air from the Gulf of Mexico resulting in the failure of summer rains. This was only part of a worldwide deterioration of climatic conditions that led to the abandonment of the cliff dwellings of the Southwest and the disappearance of village peoples across the Central Plains. At this time some of the Plains cultures became involved in the complex amalgamation of cultures known as the "Coalescent Tradition" of North and South Dakota. Many prehistoric groups lost their identity entirely and were reshaped to emerge with the developing tribes of the Historic Period. Such was the destiny of many of our western Iowa peoples.

Sources and Suggested Readings

STEED KISKER

SHIPPEE, J.M. (1941), Hopewellian and Middle Mississippi Remains from the Kansas City Area. Missouri Archaeologist, Vol. 7, No. 2, pp. 28-32.

WEDEL, WALDO R. (1943), Archaeological Investigations in Platte and Clay Counties, Missouri. U.S. National Museum Bulletin 183.

CAMBRIA

KNUDSON, RUTH ANN (1967), Cambria Village Ceramics. Plains Anthropologist, Vol. 12, No. 37, pp. 247-299.

WATRALL, CHARLES R. (1968), An Analysis of the Bone, Stone and Shell Materials from the Cambria Focus. Master's Thesis, University of Minnesota, Minneapolis.

OVER FOCUS

HURT, WESLEY R. (1951), Report of the Investigation of the Swanson Site, 39BR16, Brule County, South Dakota. Archaeological Studies Circular, No. 3, State Archaeological Commission. Pierre.

OVER, W.H. and E.E. MELEEN (1941), A Report of the Investigations of the Brandon Village Site and the Split Rock Creek Mounds. Archaeological Studies Circular, No. 3, University of South Dakota, Vermillion.

STERNS CREEK and MISSOURI BLUFFS

KEYES, CHARLES R. (1949), Four Iowa Archaeologies with Plains Affiliations. Proceedings of the 5th Plains Conference for Archaeology, Notebook No. 1, pp. 96-97. Lincoln.

TIFFANY, JOE A. (1971), The Sterns Creek Phase in Iowa. Honors Thesis, University of Iowa. Iowa City.

ST. HELENA

COOPER, PAUL (1937), Archaeology of Certain Sites in Cedar County, Nebraska. Chapters in Nebraska Archaeology, Vol. 1, No. 1. Lincoln.

An Uncertain Future

This book may give the reader the false impression that we know more about western Iowa prehistory than we really do. Much of what has been said here is speculative—offered to make the story interesting and show the potential of different approaches. The fact is that we do not have all the answers by any means. Less than one percent of the 29,000 square miles in the western counties of Iowa have ever been systematically investigated—even to record sites. Only a handful of the known sites have seen even the most superficial salvage, let alone controlled scientific investigation. We have a strong need for basic archeological research. It is expensive, time-consuming and requires special knowledge and the support of experts in at least a dozen fields.

Preservation problems are aggravated by the fact that construction projects, farm improvements, dam building, stream erosion and the like are destroying prehistoric sites at an alarming rate. Another real obstacle is the looter or "pothunter." These individuals destroy archeological sites by digging either for the sake of curiosity or to obtain "relics" for sale or trade. What is the solution to the preservation problem? Some would say legislation. Create a state antiquities law that would make it illegal for construction projects to destroy sites and looters to loot. Unfortunately it is not that simple. Most "hands off" legislation is difficult to enforce. The kinds of laws most helpful are those that foster archeological research and salvage by placing the financial burden on the agencies responsible for damage to sites. Some federal laws are like this, but states, counties and cities must cooperate and enact laws on all levels to prevent the loss of our resources just as they would act to protect the air, the streams, or any other aspect of the environment.

Education is probably the best approach of all. If people know something about the past and come to appreciate its significance they will help to preserve rather than destroy the knowledge that rightfully belongs to all people for all time. But what can the public do to help prevent the loss of our heritage? The answer depends on how much a person wants to get involved. Here are some examples:

IF YOU FIND SOMETHING: Children exploring the countryside, farmers doing spring plowing, construction workers digging a basement, all are likely to discover something sooner or later. If they inform the right people they will contribute to knowledge; if they do not they will insure that an interesting bit of the past will be destroyed forever. But whom do you tell? In Iowa there are two official contacts:

> Historic Preservation Officer
> B-13 MacLean Hall
> University of Iowa
> Iowa City, Iowa 52242

> Office of the State Archeologist
> 21 MacLean Hall
> University of Iowa
> Iowa City, Iowa 52242

IF YOU ARE A COLLECTOR: Arrowheads, scrapers, pottery, bone tools and the like — are these things of any value? Yes, if data are kept. Archeologists need to know where finds were made, when, and by whom and under what circumstances. A beautifully mounted collection of artifacts with no data is a monument to the unknown past—it insures that the people will remain unknown. An undocumented collection can contribute little toward unraveling the complex story of the past. Collectors can be of tremendous assistance particularly when artifacts are kept in the regions where they are found. That is where they are most significant.

IF YOU WANT TO CONTRIBUTE MORE: Join an amateur archeological society. Amateurs have always played an extremely important role in western Iowa archeology. They have organized research, located sites, helped with salvage and through their society activities they have interested others. If it weren't for the activities of amateurs, archeology would not have progressed nearly as far as it has.

The Iowa Archeological Society was founded in 1951. It is the state-wide organization devoted to preserving artifacts, sites and information about the past. The IAS holds an annual meeting, thus providing an opportunity for amateurs to exchange information and find out about current projects across the state. The society sponsors field trips and field schools to help members broaden their knowledge and get firsthand experience.

The state society is divided into regional chapters located in northwestern, central, south central, northeastern and southeastern Iowa. These chapters are the center for regional activities and afford the opportunity for more intensive participation. Lectures, films, field trips, salvage excavations and other special events are conducted by the chapters. For information about the Iowa Archeological Society and its affiliated chapters write to the following address:

Iowa Archeological Society

117 East Willow

Cherokee, Iowa 51012

It is well to bear in mind that not all amateur societies act in the best interests of preservation. Some include as activities artifact "fairs" held for the purpose of buying and selling "relics." Since these organizations emphasize the monetary value of specimens more than their contribution to science, any such society should be carefully avoided. Money and prehistoric artifacts do not mix any better than money and historic artifacts. One might reflect how the antique market has contributed to the loss of historical specimens and data during the last 25 years! It works the same way with archeology. In both instances, it is a waste we cannot afford.

SOME THINGS EVERYONE CAN DO:

Discourage digging for curiosity's sake—it can't do any good, but it can do a great deal of harm.

Never buy or sell an artifact. An artifact market results in data loss and further destruction of sites.

Support legislation that favors the preservation of prehistoric and early historic sites.

If something of potential importance is found in your area, make certain it is reported.

Tell your friends about the prehistory of western Iowa. Help insure that the people of the past are not always strangers!

Sources and Suggested Readings

ANDERSON, DUANE C. (1973), On Killing Artifacts. Iowa Archeoloical Society Newsletter, No. 70, pp. 4-5.

COTTER, JOHN R. (n.d.), Above Ground Archaeology. U.S. Government Printing Office. Washington, D.C.

McGIMSEY, CHARLES R. (1972), Public Archeology. Seminar Press, Inc. New York.

McGIMSEY, CHARLES R. (n.d.), Archeology and Archeological Resources: A Guide for those planning to Use, Affect, or Alter the Land's Surface. Society or American Archaeology. Washington, D.C.

McGIMSEY, CHARLES R., HESTER A. DAVIS and CARL CHAPMAN (n.d.), Stewards of the Past. Extension Division, University of Missouri, Columbia.

McMILLAN, R. BRUCE (1972), Archaeology During the Eleventh Hour. Midwest Museums Conference Quarterly, Vol. 32, No. 4, pp. 7-9.

General References

IOWA

McKUSICK, MARSHALL (1964), Men of Ancient Iowa. Iowa State University Press. Ames.

MISSOURI

CHAPMAN, CARL . and ELEANOR F. CHAPMAN (1964), Indians and Archaeology of Missouri. University of Missouri Press. Columbia.

NEBRASKA

STRONG, WILLIAM DUNCAN (1935), An Introduction to Nebraska Archaeology. Smithsonian Miscellaneous Collections, Vol. 93, No. 10

SOUTH DAKOTA

LEHMER, DONALD J. (1971), Introduction to Middle Missouri Archaeology. Anthropological Papers 1, National Park Service. Washington, D.C.

MINNESOTA

JOHNSON, ELDEN (1969), The Prehistoric Peoples of Minnesota. Minnesota Historical Society. St. Paul.

GREAT PLAINS

WEDEL, WALDO R. (1961), Prehistoric Man on the Great Plains. University of Oklahoma Press. Norman.

EASTERN WOODLANDS

GRIFFIN, JAMES B., ed. (1952), Archaeology of the Eastern United States. University of Chicago Press. Chicago.

NORTH AMERICA

CLAIBORNE, ROBERT (1973), The First Americans. Time-Life Books. New York.

JENNINGS, JESSE D. (1968), Prehistory of North America. McGraw Hill, Inc. New York.

WILLEY, GORDON R. (1966), An Introduction to American Archaeology, Vol. 1, Prentice-Hall, Inc. New York.